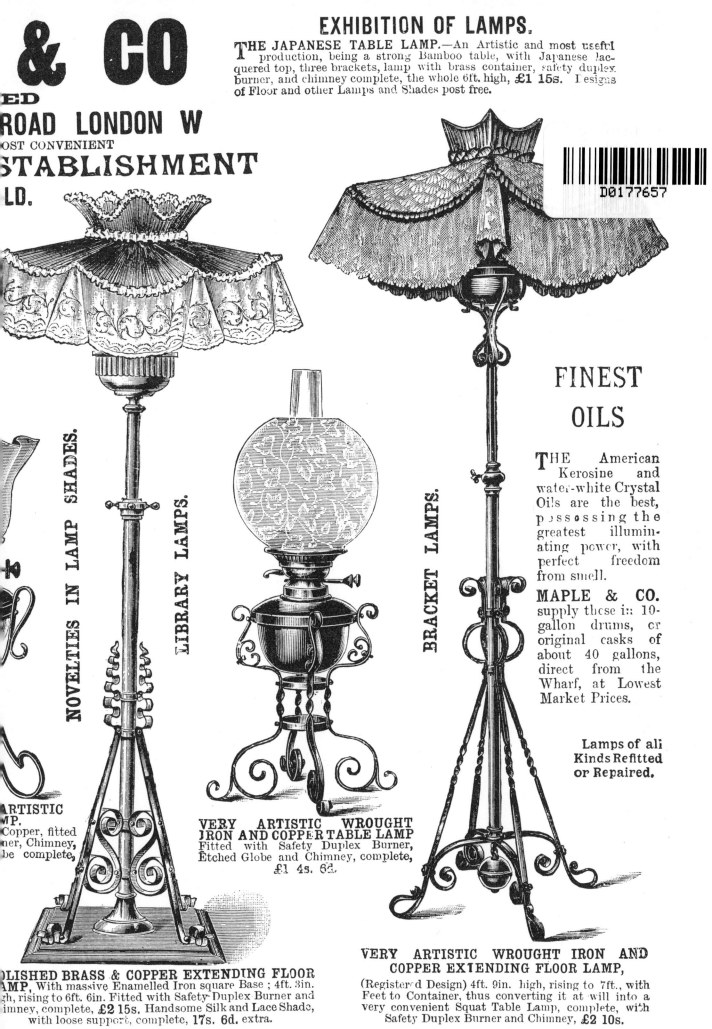

& CO

ED

ROAD LONDON W

OST CONVENIENT

STABLISHMENT

LD.

EXHIBITION OF LAMPS.

THE JAPANESE TABLE LAMP.—An Artistic and most useful production, being a strong Bamboo table, with Japanese lacquered top, three brackets, lamp with brass container, safety duplex burner, and chimney complete, the whole 6ft. high, £1 15s. Designs of Floor and other Lamps and Shades post free.

FINEST

OILS

THE American Kerosine and water-white Crystal Oils are the best, possessing the greatest illuminating power, with perfect freedom from smell.

MAPLE & CO. supply these in 10-gallon drums, or original casks of about 40 gallons, direct from the Wharf, at Lowest Market Prices.

Lamps of all Kinds Refitted or Repaired.

NOVELTIES IN LAMP SHADES.

LIBRARY LAMPS.

BRACKET LAMPS.

ARTISTIC
MP.
Copper, fitted
ner, Chimney,
be complete,

VERY ARTISTIC WROUGHT IRON AND COPPER TABLE LAMP Fitted with Safety Duplex Burner, Etched Globe and Chimney, complete, £1 4s. 6d.

OLISHED BRASS & COPPER EXTENDING FLOOR AMP, With massive Enamelled Iron square Base; 4ft. 3in. gh, rising to 6ft. 6in. Fitted with Safety Duplex Burner and imney, complete, £2 15s. Handsome Silk and Lace Shade, with loose support, complete, 17s. 6d. extra.

VERY ARTISTIC WROUGHT IRON AND COPPER EXTENDING FLOOR LAMP, (Registered Design) 4ft. 9in. high, rising to 7ft., with Feet to Container, thus converting it at will into a very convenient Squat Table Lamp, complete, with Safety Duplex Burner and Chimney, £2 10s.

D0177657

THE
WORLD
OF
VICTÖRIANA

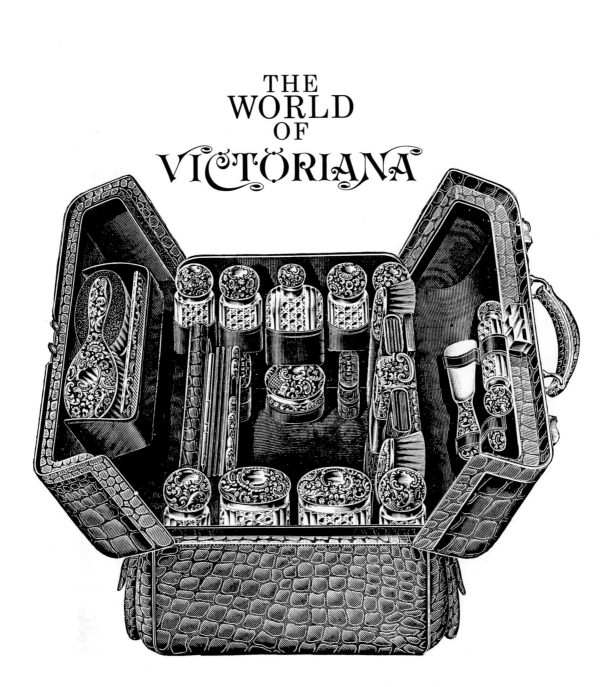

THE WORLD OF VICTORIANA

Illustrating the progress
of furniture and the decorative arts
in Britain and America from 1837 to 1901

Compiled & Written
by
JAMES NORBURY

*With over one hundred and fifty
photographs and engravings
in monochrome and colour
many of which
have been specially commissioned*

HAMLYN
London · New York · Sydney · Toronto

Dedicated to
KENNETH AND KATE TAYLOR
IN FRIENDSHIP

Title page illustration:
The Transept of the Great Exhibition.

Published by
The Hamlyn Publishing Group Limited
London · New York · Sydney · Toronto
Hamlyn House, Feltham, Middlesex, England

© copyright The Hamlyn Publishing Group Limited 1972
ISBN 0 600 39121 3

Filmset in England by Filmtype Services Limited, Scarborough
Reproduced and printed in Spain, by Printer, Industria Grafica, S.A.
Tuset 19, Barcelona, San Vicente dels Horts, 1972
Deposito Legal B. 9552–1972. Mohn-Gordon Ltd, London

Contents

Theirs was the bitterness we know
    Because the clouds of hawthorn keep
So short a state, and kisses go
    To tombs unfathomably deep,
While Rameses and Romeo
    And little Ariadne sleep.

John Drinkwater

The Bird in the Gilded Cage

Numbers in the margins refer to illustrations.

HE year was 1837. William IV, Silly Billy as some had not inappropriately nicknamed him, was dead, and a young girl had acceded to the Throne of England. An easy victim for his wiles, mused Baron Stockmar as he thought of marriage prospects for his pupil, Prince Albert of Saxe-Coburg-Gotha. A trivial, rather empty young woman, said one or two leading politicians of both Whig and Tory persuasion. An enigma, a difficult one to educate and handle said her governess, and this was to prove much more the truth than any of the other speculations.

The reign of William IV her predecessor had been noted for nothing except its dullness. He had been an easy-going monarch, a casual ruler and a nonentity as a statesman, and these things mattered at a time when constitutional monarchy signified more than it does today. Art and letters had not been encouraged by the Court and the few flowers that flourished in this garden owed everything to personal tenacity and nothing to royal patronage. To some the golden age had ended with the death of George IV; to others it had opened wide its gates with the first tremulous noises of the Industrial Revolution. To the vast majority God was still in His heaven and all was well with His world, providing one read for the word 'world' the British Empire.

We shall be wise to glance for a moment at the world as the Prince Regent, later George IV, had seen it. How did Prinny see himself? If Beau Brummel was the self-styled arbiter of elegance, he, the Prince Regent, was the undisputed judge of taste. Not for Prinny were the wide sweeps of Capability Brown landscapes, the clean lines of Hepplewhite and Sheraton, the simple splendours of Adam and Nash. It was probably Chippendale with his Oriental styles who appealed most to the Prince, and it was this influence that was to give rise to what must be seen as the Prince Regent's lasting memorial, that monstrous yet imposing building, the Royal Pavilion at Brighton. Here this strange Prince, whose mind hovered on the lunatic fringe, let loose all his extravagant desires for the unusual, the rococo and the fantastic.

The fascinating thing about Regency design is that, in spite of its sometimes overwhelming extravagance, it had as its basis an essential simplicity, at one time overlaid with a little too much ormolu, at others twisted and distorted until the result was a tortured table or a maltreated chair. Regency furniture, silver, ceramics, clothes and furnishings all shared in this desire for the extraordinary and bizarre, but, in spite of its surface contradictions, the underlying unity gave the style a meaning and purpose, and signified it as a period separate from the Georgian era that preceded it and from the Victorian age that was to follow.

We must, however, be clear on one fundamental issue. In the world of design, as in the world of aesthetics in general, one rarely finds a violent revolution, a sudden transition. The old changes and the new is born, but the legacy of the past will be an important factor in the development of the future.

*   *   *

IT was 1837. A young lady in a drawing room in Pimlico left her stool at the pianoforte and wound up the mechanism of a bird in a gilded cage, the latest 3 novelty from the Continent. The cage shone like pure gold and the bird's plumage was iridescent in the afternoon sunshine. It raised its head, its body trembled and its beak chattered as it warbled out its triumphant song. On 20th June at Kensington Palace the same young lady 1 ushered in an age where what you had and not who you were was to become the new measure of all things.

The ordinary people of England saw the first years of the new reign as heralding a new springtime.

1. 'I will be good.' *Victoria receiving the news of her accession.* By H. T. Wells, 1880. (Tate Gallery, London)

2. Queen Victoria and Prince Albert. A photograph by Roger Fenton, 1854. The Prince Consort's interest in photography was typical of his encouragement of art and technology. Roger Fenton became famous for his photographs of conditions during the Crimean campaign which stripped war of its legendary glamour. (Victoria and Albert Museum, London)

3. A bird in a gilded cage was a popular Victorian novelty often given to young ladies by their prospective husbands. When wound up the bird will sing and move.

2

3

The young girl was radiant and had her own beauty enhanced by a crown. Soon her Prince would come and the reign would turn into the semblance of one of the operettas so popular in Vienna, Paris and later in England itself.

It has been wisely said, 'Uneasy lies the head that wears a crown', but equally uneasy is the head that lies next to that crowned one and has to support it. The young Queen was a charming, vivacious but difficult woman. She was proud of her position, jealous of her royal prerogative and regal dignity. By her side, adored and devoted but duly kept in his place, was 'dear Albert', royal consort, somewhat higher than a prince but less than a monarch. The Prince Consort has been both misunderstood and misrepresented. He was not the bowing sycophant or the silent and loving husband that many have pictured him. He was a forward-looking man who saw in the industrial development around him the promise of an ever-expanding future. That future depended on trade, and that trade depended on as many people as possible seeing for themselves what Great Britain had to offer to them, and, of equal importance, what they had to offer to Great Britain. If we were to become the shop window of the world we must make

sure of two things, that our window was well stocked with goods and that those goods were what the customers wanted to buy. The new railroads, the development of shipping companies, the improvements in the mail services, all were part of a new way of life, and we in this country had to prove ourselves to be the pioneers in this as we had been in the invention and use of industrial machinery.

In the 1840s the Prince Consort had his moment of vision. He would inspire and organise a way in which all men might see for themselves the many goods we manufactured and at the same time those made overseas. There must be an exhibition, but its whole conception must be new and daring and reflect in every possible way that magic word, 'progress'. Prince Albert was, from first to last, to be the dominating influence on this, one of the greatest enterprises in the fields of commerce and industry that England had ever undertaken. He called together a committee representing various aspects of trade and industry and discussed with them his project in detail. Where should it be housed? How should it be staged so that all would be shown off to the best advantage? Possible sites were mentioned, but finally Hyde Park was selected. This

4. A great attraction at the 1851 Great Exhibition was the Albert chair. An ornate affair in carved and inlaid walnut, its special feature was a large porcelain plaque with a portrait of the Prince Consort. The Prince had been severely criticised for his sponsorship of the Great Exhibition. Prophets of doom feared that the Crystal Palace would be blown down, with tragic consequences. Worse still, it was feared that England would be overrun with villainous foreigners who would cause a famine by eating all our food, and, moreover, would spread depravity, barbarism and the Black Death throughout the land. As a result of the success of the Exhibition the Prince encouraged the setting up of a museum of manufactures, now called the Victoria and Albert Museum, where this chair is on show.

5

site, more than any other, could be called the centre of Britain and the hub of the Empire. It was large and spacious and had all the facilities needed for such a vast undertaking. Housing the exhibits was another matter. First the building must fit into the park; also it must have the maximum amount of light. A competition was run for all who were capable of designing and constructing an edifice worthy of such a magnificent occasion. Invitations were already being sent out to possible exhibitors. Diplomats were discussing the idea abroad, for it must be a universal event.

Over two hundred designs were submitted, but the winning entry was one by Joseph Paxton. Paxton had started life as a gardener and had for many years been interested in the construction of greenhouses. In 1837 he had designed the great glasshouse at Chatsworth, covering an acre of ground, to house the Duke of Devonshire's orchids. His winning entry was no more than a gigantic greenhouse, a structure of iron and glass that was to make people who saw it gasp with surprise and astonishment. It was like the fantastic concept of an Oriental magician, and when completed – it was erected in only seventeen weeks – stood towering in the park reflecting every change of light and shade of the passing clouds. Its dimensions were an unbelievable 1,848 feet long and 456 feet wide, a vast area of glass in an iron frame supported by over 600 columns. Its baptism was carried out by that well-loved, satirical weekly journal, *Punch*, who christened it the Crystal Palace. One has to admit that it could not have been better named.

On 1st May, 1851, with pageantry worthy of such 122 an auspicious occasion, the Great Exhibition was regally opened by Queen Victoria herself, accompanied by her husband. Inside the glass case, for it looked like a huge display cabinet, were pagodas from China, mosques from India, temples from Ceylon and native huts from Africa, each section reflecting a national heritage as well as exhibiting that country's wares. Pottery and porcelain, mandarin coats and kimonos, silks and muslins, ebonies and ivories, precious and semi-precious stones, carved masks and wooden idols, totem poles, boomerangs and sheepskin rugs, these were but a few items which represented in riotous fashion the Queen's dominions overseas.

From Great Britain itself, well, it is no cliché to say, 'You name it, they had it', for all the human skill and ingenuity of both industrialist and craftsman had been prevailed upon. It was the golden noonday of the Queen's reign and never again was it to be equalled, let alone surpassed. All the leading china and pottery factories were represented, with glazed earthenware and figures and statuettes in the novel parian ware simulat- 21 ing marble. There were fireplaces and fancy pillars, ornamental wrought-iron work lamps and lanterns, clocks, firearms and barometers. Even the most casual glance through the pages of the illustrated catalogue reveals the depth and breadth of mind of organiser and exhibitor alike.

One aspect of the exhibition has a particular bearing on our story; this was the new look it gave to English furniture. The beloved four-poster beds were lighter, delicately carved with traceries on pillars, canopies and sides. Chairs assumed a comfort and elegance that brought them into line with the great tradition of British craftsmanship. Tables were finer, flimsier and more delicate in design and treatment. True, one or two of the pianos were too highly decorated with inlays and imitation marquetry, and some of the display cabinets were like miniatures of the Crystal Palace itself.

6

5,6

The mistress of the house also found plenty to interest her on the stands: new wallpapers and curtain drapes, flower-pots and vases, ornaments and tea-cosies in ivory and silver. For those who liked the small and decorative there were carved ebony elephants with ivory tusks, brasses from Benares and jewelled caskets from Ceylon. There were discreetly draped female statues for the garden, wrought-iron tables and chairs for the conservatory, miniature pagodas for gazebos and summer-houses, gates and railings, fenders, kitchen sinks and washboilers, and so the gigantic catalogue goes on. This was everybody's day out, and it is no exaggeration to say that the World and his Wife were to be found from Monday to Saturday sauntering through Hyde Park to the cascade of iron and glass that beckoned them into its tempting portals.

Great Britain was at this time becoming more and more aware of her export trade. On many of the porcelain stands were plates specifically designed for the American market and depicting American scenes like the White House, Palm Beach, Miami or the Gulf of Mexico. As an added inducement to prospective buyers, if they ordered in quantity they could have their own name and details of the illustration printed on the back. The day of the souvenir had dawned.

The Great Exhibition had given a great deal of pleasure to the Queen. Was it not a moment of true glory for her beloved Albert? The fact that the genius of Joseph Paxton and the skills of thousands of designers and craftsmen, together with the changing aspects of travel and transport, had done as much to further the exhibition's success as her husband's moment of vision that had led to its inception was outside her comprehension. She was a middle-aged romantic, a Queen whose dignity and decorum upheld and maintained the hypo-

5,6. Souvenir plates. On the left, the Florida State Plate issued in celebration of the founding of the State of Florida in 1845. The mark records that the plate was 'Made in Staffordshire, England, by the Adams Potteries established 1657' and that it was 'Designed and imported exclusively by the World famous Robert Lewis Art Galleries, St Petersburg, Florida'. (Private collection) On the right is a plate made by Samuel Acock and Company for the 1851 Great Exhibition showing the flags of the participating countries. (Private collection)

crisy of Victorian life. If anyone deviated from her strict observance of morality, she was not amused.

The Exhibition also had far-reaching consequences on the lives of the wealthy middle classes. They had walls knocked out and conservatories added, windows enlarged and French windows built in. Their furniture became lighter, daintier and gayer in every way. Representatives from pottery firms, they were not yet called commercial travellers, called with their charming miniature samples of glass, china, Staffordshire figures, even pieces of furniture. These travellers' samples must not be confused with the fittings and furnishings of dolls' houses. They were in essence the Victorian world in miniature and are much sought after by collectors today.

10,11
57

*   *   *

ON 14th December, 1861, the Prince Consort died of typhoid fever. The Queen was distraught. The morning star and midday sun had been swept away. Hitherto she had leaned on him for everything; now she was alone and bereft; all that lay ahead was an endless waste of years. She would retire from it all. The tomb had imprisoned her beloved, and she would willingly

9 incarcerate herself at Osborne. Later Windsor Castle would become once again a monarch's fortress; her protection from the intruding world which would look in idle curiosity at her sorrow. Although her subjects were moved and distressed by Albert's death they could not see it as the end of the world. The unwritten creed of the Victorians was the inviolability of progress, and all around was ample witness to this claim. The same people who had cheered her before Albert's death were ready to boo and cat-call her name when she withdrew in lonely and desolate seclusion to Windsor. At first her sorrow had commanded respect, but her constant refusal to take any interest in her country or people led to feelings of republicanism. The fear of Parliament became so great that the Government demanded her return to the capital and her appearance before the people. Under pressure she condescended to do so, and perhaps saved her country from being thrust to the edge of a political revolution.

She might flirt with Mr Disraeli, dislike Mr Gladstone, but she never succeeded in knowing anything vital about the lives and well-being, or lack of well-being, of the common people. They liked her eldest son, Teddy. In his rakish and raffish ways there was much in his character that appealed to them. Their lives were brightened by gossip and scandal, and a Prince of Wales who gave rise to so much scandal, although frowned upon by Church and State, was to a certain extent idolised by the working classes. To the men he was simply one of the boys; to the women he was one of the men they might have had a dalliance with had they moved in the right stratum of society.

The young lady in the Pimlico drawing room had become a wrinkled old woman; the gilded bird cage had 156 become tarnished; the bird had lost its plumage; and, as the tired spring uncoiled itself, the bird spluttered and gurgled as it swayed unsteadily on its perch. It was the forgotten toy of half a century ago. Soon it would be swept away; the high song would be over, and the nouveaux riches of an Edwardian Age would sing out loudly and clearly the vulgar and vibrant music-hall songs of their day.

7. Silver inkstand. Most Victorian designers thought that 'art' must be ornate or picturesque. Such theories lay behind the design of this 'artistic' silver inkstand composed of an apple, a pear and a pomegranate on a vine-leaf base. (Victoria and Albert Museum, London)

8. "The Subject's Best Friend". The Victorians saw nothing incongruous in linking the Queen with something as humble as soap powder. The combination of snobbery and sentiment has proved to be an enduringly successful advertising device.

7

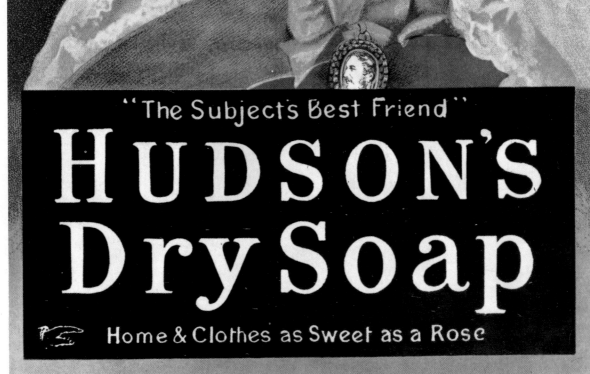

"The Subject's Best Friend"

HUDSON'S Dry Soap

Home & Clothes as Sweet as a Rose

8

9. Queen Victoria's sitting room, Osborne House, Isle of Wight. After Albert's tragic death, the Queen retired in inconsolable grief to Osborne, the palace where they had spent so many happy hours. In the sitting room their simple twin desks remain, cluttered with family photographs. The balloon-back chairs, the side tables, the gilt-framed paintings, the ornaments under glass domes and the floral carpet were typical of many Victorian upper middle-class homes.

10. A case of glass toys for young ladies and travellers' samples. Actual size of case: 16 in × 12 in. (Private collection)

11. Group of china miniatures and travellers' samples. Actual size of case: 27 in × 14½ in. (Private collection)

11

The Victorian Age

ANY a river starts with a trickle and ends with a torrent. This might well be said of the stream of progress from the years 1800 to 1850. For the new industrial magnates it was an age of development and prosperity. Trade was booming. New routes were opening for Britain's expanding exports, and consignments of all kinds of goods were reaching her shores from foreign climes. Spices from the Orient, exotic plants from tropical zones, birds and beasts from faraway places were all finding their way into the Victorian home. Grey parrots from Africa, brightly plumaged macaws from South America, marmosets and small monkeys were found as household pets alongside the familiar dog and the neglected cat. Sometimes the parrots disclosed a strange and unseemly vocabulary; then they were either despatched to a zoo or expelled to the cook's or gardener's quarters.

As far as the British Empire was concerned it moved, like the God it worshipped, in a mysterious way, with gun in one hand and bible in the other. It would tame the savage beast and make it the willing or unwilling slave of the British Raj. The British were convinced that even if they had not arrived at Utopia they were well on the way to it, and if there were malcontents what did they matter in the golden age into which the country was entering.

If I were asked to define in a single word what made the Victorian age stand apart from its predecessors, that word would be 'money'. Taste was to be dethroned and the rattling of the cash till was to take its place. The promise of 1837 was to be lost in the shadows of 1937, a hundred years' span that saw the rise and fall of the British Empire, the only empire on which the sun was not allowed to set.

In 1837 a new generation was coming into being.

The age of the aristocrat was declining, the French Revolution had been a violent reminder of this fact, and the day of the merchant banker and industrialist was dawning. It was this factor more than any other that was to make, mould and mar the new age. Why should anyone worry about the bankruptcy of taste when the banknotes of the industrialists were piling up in counting houses all over Europe and America? Machines had come to stay in spite of the protests of the Luddites; the age of steam lay just ahead; and at the end of the Victorian era we were to see the first horseless carriages. Not only was speed to become our God, but the speeding up of everything was to lead to what some saw as the pathway to the golden age and others viewed as the road to destruction.

Unless we view the Victorian period against this background, we shall fail to grasp the significance of its art and design. Vulgarity and vainglory were destined to triumph despite the pleas of John Ruskin for a return to ancient splendours, and the cries of William Morris and his followers for us not to destroy the true creative nature and needs of the human spirit. There were to be moments of beauty, occasions when taste conquered the desire for vulgarity. In the middle years of the era, the French influence of the Second Empire, and the brilliant work of individual designers in furniture, glass, silver and ceramics were to have their place, but a few solitary aesthetic swallows could not make an elegant summer. The main criterion among the rising industrial class was how much did it cost, and the urbane delight of the new middle class was to ape in slightly more vulgar terms the ideas and ways of their betters. What use was the visionary world of William Blake in the nightmare realm of banknotes and pawnshops?

One of the most interesting facts of the period is that it had little impact on the titled families who still

12. Sir John Tenniel, of *Alice in Wonderland* fame, was chief cartoonist of *Punch* from 1864.

JUSTICE—FOR IRELAND.

13. Stuffed birds, a pictorial serving jug, a brass-bound bible, a papier-mâché inkstand, ivory needlework tools; all these typically Victorian objects display the longing for the picturesque which characterises the period.

14. Bookmarks. Centre: cut paper on blue ribbon. Left and right: two of woven silk, one still on its original mount. (Private collection)

13

regarded themselves as the backbone of England. It is true that towards the end of the century their younger sons were going into commerce, and their daughters might marry into one of the better-known families of the new middle class. But in the main they lived as they had done for centuries, calmly slumbering among the thunderous noises of change, secure, or so they thought, in their dreams of past feudal splendour. They had made few concessions to the changing face of England and the new ideas offered little to interest them. They still lived in their halls and manor houses surrounded by the possessions their families had collected through the centuries. Here were treasures of an earlier and more refined age. Sèvres, Rockingham, Dresden and Viennese porcelain, gold and silver plate, Hepplewhite, Sheraton and Chippendale furniture, these were all the real thing and not the shoddier imitations that were to abound in the Victorian era. They might have added a chiffonier, a pair of wine coolers, a new draped and decorated four-poster bed, more paintings to hang on their walls and pieces of sculpture for their gardens and terraces. If they sought to embody the spirit of the age they would change to the Italian style of gardening and add a few follies to decorate their grounds. But in the main they were like the God they worshipped, the same yesterday and today and, they hoped, forever.

However, the social structure was changing; not only were the daughters of the aristocracy marrying into trade, industry and commerce, but the younger sons who had failed to gain commissions in the army or to find suitable livings in the Church were likewise looking to the new industrial order for positions. Nevertheless, the Grand Tour was still considered an essential part of every good education, and so porcelain

65 from Germany and France, glass from Italy and copies of well-known 18th-century ceramics from the clever

77 hands of Mr Samson were soon to find their place in every home worthy of that name. Possessions, posses-

13 sions and still more possessions, these were the outward and visible signs of that state of grace which every Victorian father sought to attain. Not who he was but what he had was to become the new social criterion, and many a family who might have been frowned upon and dismissed as 'trade' in the early years of the century was to find its offspring moving in the highest circles; being honoured by the Crown; and, in one or two cases, taking a seat in the House of Lords.

The Victorian middle classes were probably the most perfect examples of arrogance and hypocrisy who ever disgraced the pages of history. It is of them that Llewelyn Powys said, 'It is easy enough to get into the middle classes, the difficult thing is to get out of them.'

140 Staffordshire portrait figures of the Queen and her family graced their mantel-shelves; plaques of Mr and Mrs Gladstone hung on each side. Their coffins were of heavy oak with silver-plated or brass fittings, and covered with a silver-encrusted and embroidered black velvet pall. Middle-class Victorian monuments still grace our churches, beneath middle-class Victorian stained glass. The subjects for stained glass were senti-

mental in the extreme. If an artist was bold enough to show Adam and Eve in their primal innocence before the Fall they might not be wearing a fig leaf but their whole bodies, except hands and feet, heads and shoulders, would be hidden behind the tree itself. Coy Eves would offer the reddest apples to frightened Adams; Ruth and Naomi would simper like a couple of milkmaids at the well; Job would look the epitome of despair as he looked up in vain to heaven for mercy; and the Infant Jesus looked very much like the cherubic child in the picture of *Bubbles* that made a fortune for one well-known soap manufacturer of the time. Convinced of their mission, the middle classes tore down the past and replaced it with their over-ornamented, sentimental and pretentious present.

The rooms of the middle classes underwent many changes. By mid century the dining room had sporting prints upon the walls. In the library we might find

15

copies of some of Hogarth's more respectable prints, and on the shelves had been added the works of Surtees and that rather startling Mr Ruskin, whose opinions on art were infallible but whose social ideas seemed a little out of keeping with his age. But then he could be excused because he lived among artists and all artists were a little bit peculiar and did not quite fit into the mode of the time. On the walls of the drawing room were small miniatures, water-colours, more prints and the fashionable silhouettes. The walls were so full of such items that little of the wall itself, at least beneath the picture rail, could be seen.

There were chairs, whatnots, stools and tables everywhere so that a drawing room of the sixties resembled an overcrowded and far too exuberant Eastern bazaar. Pot plants and palms stood in every bay. It was a cluttered age where every inch of space had something to fill it.

16

15. Cameo vase designed by Thomas Woodall and decorated by J. T. Fereday at Thomas Webb and Sons, Stourbridge, first exhibited 1884. The carving of layered glass had its heyday in the 1880s when exquisitely carved vases and plaques were made for a wealthy and exclusively English clientele. (Victoria and Albert Museum, London)

16. Three glasses. Part of a table service designed by Philip Webb for William Morris in 1859. Their functional simplicity sets them apart from the ornate cut and engraved glass of the period. Such courageous experiments have proved to be the foundations of modern design. (Victoria and Albert Museum, London)

Feathers built up like sprays of flowers, stuffed 17 birds standing on perilous twigs in bowers of artificial foliage, wax flowers, all would be seen under glass domes in every room of the house. This mania for collecting and never thinning out was the menace of the period. Some years ago I saw a drawing room in a private house that had made no concessions to the changing years and was furnished as it had been in 1884. I counted over fifty pictures, photographs, silhouettes, and pressed flowers on the walls, while on the tables and mantel-shelves were twenty-two domes of wax fruit, flowers, feathery pieces of nonsense and stuffed birds. As if this were not enough there was a stuffed Amazon parrot in a brass cage that one expected at any moment to shriek out 'To hell with it all'.

Middle-class ladies were always busy, knitting lace in fine cotton, crocheting, working cross-stitch embroideries in brightly coloured Berlin wools, and making all kinds of things in bead-work and in the 84 newly introduced and extremely popular macramé, or 95 the art of creative knotting. Their prolific output flourished on antimacassars, trays, bags, footstools and 9 chair seats, decorated for their aesthetic significance rather than comfort, and on fire-screens, slipper boxes by the fender, and face-screens to protect the delicate 84,100 feminine skin from the heat of the winter fire.

Curtains, pelmets, drapes and hangings, 'veritable dust traps' to the housemaid, were everywhere. Windows were shrouded in the new lace curtains, the pride of the Nottingham manufacturers. Macramé drapes were superseded by silk damask curtains, and muslin waterfalls kept the light from entering the room. For light and fresh air were considered the enemies of good health. It was inconceivable that a tightly laced waistline encased in steel ribbed stays led to constipation, indigestion and the vapours, the three most common ailments of the Victorian household.

One good thing had happened in the mid Victorian transformation: the heavy furniture of twenty years before had disappeared. Walnut, satinwood and rosewood were much used, and tables and chairs took on the delicate lace-like forms of an earlier period. Just as in our own day we are seeing a revival of Georgian and Regency reproductions, so too the Victorians based their designs on the ideas of Sheraton, Chippendale and 18,102 Hepplewhite. I say 'based on' for even here the age had to make its mark; some pieces were painted or overemphasised by inlays, or had that extra twist or curl to mar the original simple statement of design.

In the case of glass, pottery and porcelain, the demand far exceeded the supply and we had the first signs of slipshod work from lesser-known factories, while the well-known ones would strive to reproduce past elegance, altered a little to fit in with present trends.

At the lower end of the social scale, the life of tenant farmers and cottage dwellers who lived on great estates was straightforward, and moved through the passage of the seasons with the stately solemnity of a tolling bell. They possessed their lovely pine dressers,

17. Ornaments under glass domes. The *Greek Slave*, the most popular parian statuette of the age, surrounded by bouquets made from wool, wax, skeleton leaves, feathers and silk on wire frames. (Private collection)

fruitwood chairs, and oak refectory tables, simple but elegant furniture made by village craftsmen who had seen the fine furnishings of their feudal lords. But the agricultural workers fared badly. They were forced to live on a pittance that hardly kept them alive, and if they died of starvation there was always the village doctor, who drank port with the squire, to say that they died of natural causes. His words were true, for in their life of penury to die of lack of food and warmth was common enough. Complaint meant eviction, and eviction meant the poorhouse; few wanted to face this.

49 To these people the industrial age gave new hope, and many flocked to the newly developing towns where work was plentiful if pay was poor. It was here they were gradually to learn the lessons of their secret weapon: labour power. At first the industrialists had their own way, but in the 1830s the plight of children dying under looms from sheer drudgery and overwork led Lord Shaftsbury to fight for the first of many Factory Acts. A new radicalism was arising, and by the second half of the century another revolutionary idea, Socialism, was coming to birth. Its pioneers were largely inspired by the Nonconformists, while the High Anglicans in the Established Church were talking airily about the dignity of man and the labourer being worthy of his hire.

It was from this rising tide of discontent that the trade unions came into being. These things were just as much part of the Victorian age as were the hundred and one objects with which the wealthy cluttered up their rooms.

We cannot leave our review of the Victorian social scene without mentioning two things that enlivened the dreary lives of the workers. One was the rise of the popular public-house entertainers which later gave birth to the music hall. The other was the importation from Germany of the crude, bawdy groups of figures 23,24 that are known as fairings. Fairings deserve a book to themselves. They started with the country swains buying ribbons for their girl friends at the annual fairs and are immortalised in the old song *Oh dear what can the matter be*. They then developed into the cheap pottery figures and groups that were on sale at fair grounds, whose roundabouts and swings were becoming a popular sight in all parts of the country. The towns might have developed and spread, but the fairs that linked them to their rural origins still persisted, and it was on stalls at these fairs that fairings could be purchased for a few pence. They were crude and often satirical and in a very rough way provided a social commentary on some aspects of the time. They preceded the comic postcard and are of the same genre. *Looking Down on his Luck*, a bewildered father gazing down at a snug little cradle containing triplets or twins; *Sarah's Young Man*, a follower hiding under the tablecloth when he hears the mistress approaching; *Wedding Night*, an anxious bridegroom unfastening his wife's stays; *The Power of Love*, a husband seen kissing the housemaid while his wife is approaching from another room; these are but a few of the many subjects dealt with in these delightful

18. Mid Victorian neo-Gothic tea table of amboyna wood with zebra wood details. The multi-column legs and fretwork brackets are the so-called Gothic motifs. (Private collection)

sidelights on an age. There were also those more suitable to grace the mantel-shelves of the children's bedrooms such as *Little Boy Blue* and *Red Riding Hood*, and pieces for the proud mother or grandmother like *Baby's First Step* or *Children Meeting*. Fairings flooded the market in their thousands from the 1880s to the close of the century.

The Victorians might clutter their walls with prints and pictures; cover their shelves with stuffed 84 birds and wax flowers; their cupboards might be filled 13,17 to overflowing with glass, china, and silver; their dressing tables might sag with the load of knick-nacks, pin boxes and cushions, ring-holders, hair-tidies and the 22,120 like; these were to them symbols of the two factors that dominated their lives: a sense of growing opulence, and a growing fear of insecurity. Already in the industrial north of England wags were saying, 'from riches to rags in three generations'.

19. Tête-à-tête sofa from an early Victorian book of designs. The ingenuity of the design with its little centre table appealed to the Victorian love of novelty.

20. The Chevy Chase sideboard. Made by Gerrard Robinson of Newcastle, 1857–1863. A number of elaborately carved sideboards were made in England in the 1850s and 60s depicting narrative scenes from epics of history and romance. Here in six panels are scenes from the ballad of Chevy Chase. The sideboard is now at the Grosvenor Hotel, Shaftesbury.
(Trust Houses Limited)

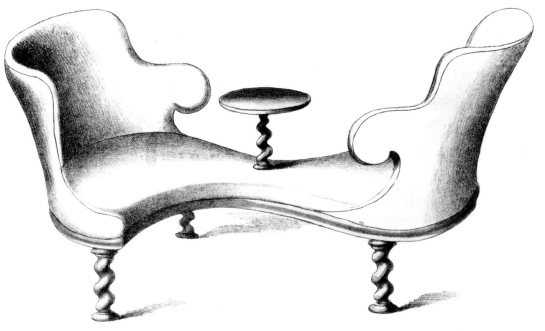

21. *Naomi and her daughters-in-law.* Minton parian statuary with Great Exhibition mark. Parian is a translucent creamy-white porcelain invented at the Copeland factory in 1842. Parian groups and portrait busts were extremely popular in Britain throughout the Victorian period; the finest are those by Copeland and Minton. (Author's collection)

22. Group of silver ornaments and pin cushions. The Victorians excelled at producing decorative knick-knacks of all kinds and qualities. These well-executed silver animals are typical of this craft. (Private collection)

23,24. Victorian fairings. These pottery ornaments, captioned groups, spice holders, match holders and pin boxes, were originally made in German factories and imported to England to be sold at country fairs. Small Staffordshire fairground ornaments began to be made from 1895 onwards. (Author's collection)

25. Doulton salt-glazed stoneware mug and biscuit barrel etched by William and Hannah Barlow. (Private collection)

21

22

28

23

24

25

Hands across the sea

ORKING conditions all over Europe were one of the major scandals of the 19th century. By 1875, conditions among many of the agricultural workers and some of the new working classes in the factories had become desperate. Wages were low, but labour was plentiful and anything was better than the alternatives of vagrancy or the workhouse; in fact many men and women worked for wages that kept them far below the subsistence level. Many poor families faced with a desolate future were drawn to the New World. Irish, Italians, Germans, Jews, the Scots and the Welsh, all sought a new life across the Atlantic. They travelled in conditions worse than those provided for the cattle that were slaughtered to provide food for them en route. The new Steam Packet Line was doing a profitable business and could offer low fares to these poor creatures who had little to hope for if they remained behind. America was a land of new enterprises, of new endeavours. Not only the poor made the journey but some of the wealthier middle-class families also decided to make a fresh start in the land of opportunities.

29

All the emigrants, rich and poor, took with them their precious possessions, from a houseful of furniture to an odd piece of pottery, a simple item of furniture, copper and brass kettles and pans. They were to find on arrival much that reminded them of the old country.

A number of craftsmen joined the stream of immigrants and established themselves and their workshops in the New World. Many stayed in New York but some were to venture inland and to the south.

112

30

Meanwhile, trade was increasing rapidly between the Old and New Worlds. The more adventurous traders on both sides of the Atlantic paid sales visits across the ocean to increase the outlets for their products. American stores imported pottery and porcelain from Staffordshire, Dresden, Paris and Vienna, cut glass from Ireland and coloured glass from Bristol and Bohemia, much of which was being designed especially for the new American market; while in return Europe imported pottery, glass and furniture from America.

31

An interesting episode occurred when a pioneer of mass-produced clocks in America, Chauncey Jerome, tried importing his clocks to England at the extremely competitive landed price of $1.50 (about 7s 6d). The British Government, determined to protect the home trade, accused Jerome of dumping, and promptly bought up the lot. Delighted, Jerome proceeded to send an even larger consignment, which the British Government again bought up in its entirety. The tenacious Jerome eventually won through and his clocks were soon being sold at 17s 6d.

America also pioneered pressed glass, the cheap imitation of expensive cut glass which threatened the traditional sources of European glass manufacture. American pressed glass, according to an Englishman returning from New York, 'was far superior, both in design and execution, to anything of the kind I had ever seen in London or elsewhere. The merit of this invention is due to the Americans; and it is likely to prove one of great national importance.'

32

It is worth remembering that the availability of a wide range of goods at all prices occurred only with the progress of the Industrial Revolution. In earlier periods fine things of all descriptions were commissioned but could be seen only in the great houses. The plutocracy of Great Britain and America ordered a set of chairs, a dining table, an elegant carved bed, a complete suite of silver and set of porcelain for use at table. It was not simply how much it cost but what it looked like that mattered. Even if they were not all men of taste themselves, they could afford to satisfy their whims for the nearest to perfection that their age had to offer by em-

26. Moorish smoking room in John D. Rockefeller's New York City house, *c.* 1880. (Brooklyn Museum, New York)

27. Although a large amount of Bohemian glass was imported into the United States from the 1820s onwards, this covered vase in ruby and clear overlay cut glass is an example of American-made Bohemian glass, manufactured by the New England Glass Company in about 1845. Its simple design and classical elegance distinguish it from the more elaborate imported ware. (The Toledo Museum of Art, Toledo, Ohio, Gift of Dr Frank W. Gunsaulus)

28. Tiffany and Company created this enamelled silver vase for the World's Columbian Fair of 1893. This truly American piece is quite unique and shows a deal of national pride: its form is taken from the relics of the ancient cliff-dwellers of the Pueblos; the eight handles are Toltec and represent the early Americans; the decorations are composed of plants representative of the north, south, east and west of America. (The Metropolitan Museum of Art, New York; Gift of Mrs Winthrop Atwell)

29. The grand saloon of the *Great Eastern*. Wood engraving from the *Illustrated London News* of 15th October, 1859. Founded in 1842, the *I.L.N.* was the first modern popular illustrated periodical. The problem of producing a large number of illustrations quickly for a long print run (the circulation in the 1850s was in the region of 60,000 copies) meant the use of multiple wood blocks, often engraved by a number of artists who worked to a uniform style that would stand up to hard wear. Thus we see art subordinated to the machine in the interest of mass production.

27

28

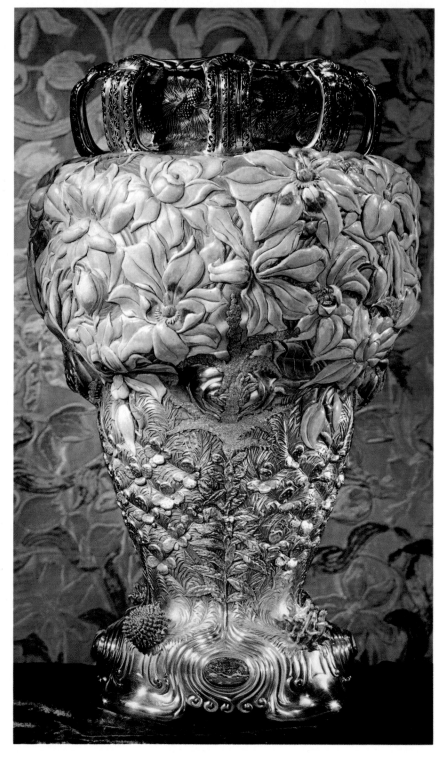

29

ploying architects, landscape gardeners, silversmiths and cabinetmakers to advise them on matters of good taste. Their portraits and those of their houses, dogs, mistresses and horses were all commissioned and painted by acknowledged masters. Since money was of little object they were able to capture the perfection of the age in which they lived.

We should not, however, dismiss and condemn the products of the Victorian age because they were mass produced. We must recall that Sheraton, Hepplewhite, Adam and Chippendale were all men who saw mass production in their own time as part of the method of producing furniture. Some would produce chair arms, others legs. Chippendale himself even imported the parts from France and tried to smuggle them into the country to pass off as products of his own workshop. The criterion was not how they were produced but the method by which their production was planned, supervised and passed as being worthy of the master craftsmen who had been their creators. The joiners, turners, woodcarvers, glassmakers, potters, and silversmiths of the 18th century all fulfilled the edict of Eric Gill that 'the artist is not a special kind of man but every man is a special kind of artist'. The second-rate and shoddy were never glossed over or tarted up; they were cast aside. It was a world in which we saw the reality of order; all things were assembled together for their in-

herent beauty, and this beauty was in a single joint or an elaborate piece of furniture, in the perfect line of a silver spoon or the detailed design of a punch-bowl carrying the armorial bearings of its proud owner.

The Industrial Revolution in Britain and America not only changed the pace of mining, spinning, weaving and the many other processes that had hitherto been largely the field of individual craftsmen; machine power 29 also offered new opportunities to manufacturers to bring mass-produced goods into thousands of ordi- 31, 32 nary homes. In every town furniture-makers sprang up 34 to meet the ever-increasing demand for more and more things, a demand that was now starting to come from the middle classes who were beginning to share in a small way their masters' prosperity. It is true that many of these furniture-makers had no conception of design and turned out badly executed imitations of either earlier pieces or the work of their superiors. Their inferior work was made to look much better by use of inlays and veneers. There were, however, a few master-craftsmen, and it is their work that gives to Victorian furniture some of the prestige it is starting to enjoy today.

English furniture of the Victorian age falls into two general groups: historical revivals and progressive. The Victorian period witnessed a series of revivals from Classical to Rococo, Elizabethan, Gothic and Renais- 42 sance, in that order. The finest pieces of Victorian historical revival furniture were produced by firms like Gillow's, Holland's and Wright and Mansfield. The second, much smaller, progressive group centres on a few reformers starting with Pugin and continuing through Ruskin and William Morris who campaigned for a return to simplicity and function, although they cannot be said to have escaped the trap of revivalism themselves. Morris's ideals inspired the establishment of the Arts and Crafts Movement by a group of leading designers committed to fighting against the excesses of historical revivals and the lowering of standards as a result of inferior mass production. The firms of Heal and Son, Schoolbred, and Jackson and Graham are notable for their support of Arts and Crafts ideals. The most vociferous member of the movement was Charles Lock Eastlake whose *Hints on Household Taste*, first published in 1868 and reprinted many times, had widespread influence in England and America.

Victorian furniture in America was influenced both by imported European styles and by immigrant craftsmen from Britain, France and Germany, as a result of which it developed along similar but not identical lines as furniture in Europe.

America's first furniture pattern book, *The Cabinet Maker's Assistant*, was compiled by John Hall and published in 1840. The designs were based on the French Restoration style. During the following twenty years, Gothic revival furniture became fashionable, its greatest exponent being the architect Alexander Jackson Davis. The German-born John Henry Belter, the outstanding figure of American Victorian furniture, led the popular mid century Rococo revival. The delicacy of the Rococo style in turn gave way to the ponderous Renaissance and Louis XVI revivals, the latter introduced by the Paris-New York firm of Ringuet-Le Prince and Marcotte.

Following the Philadelphia Centennial Exposition of 1876, nostalgia for Colonial furniture swept the country and reproductions of 18th-century pieces were made in great quantity. In the 1880s the fashion was for Orientalia, epitomised by John D. Rockefeller's splendid smoking room in the Turkish manner. The craze for exotic styles reached its height in the 1890s when elements from quite different archaeological sources were freely amalgamated in the same piece. The effect was occasionally charming, but more often hideous.

In contrast to all these revivals was the furniture

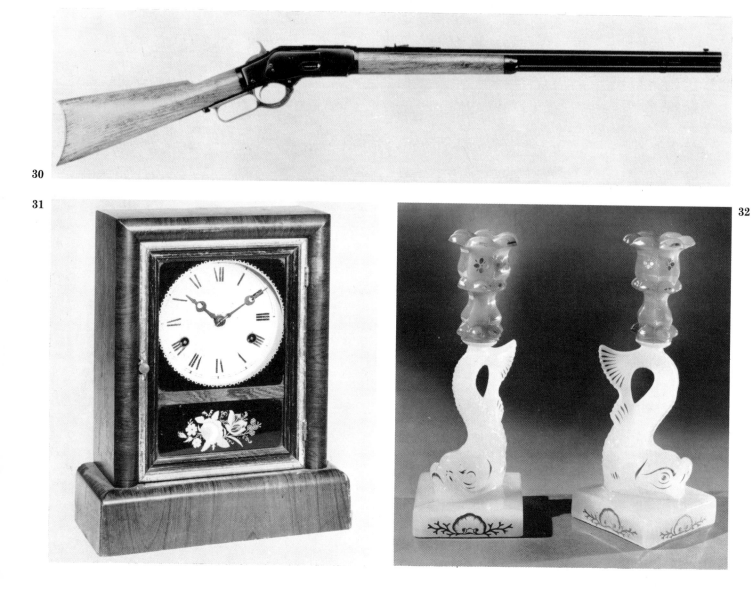

30. The 1873 model of the Winchester repeating rifle was steel framed with a lever action and took fifteen centre-fire cartridges. Its speed and accuracy made it the ideal weapon for American pioneers in hostile country, and it has been affectionately called 'the gun that won the West'. (Winchester Gun Museum, New Haven, Conn.)

31. American shelf clock. America pioneered cheap mass-produced clocks for the working-class market and exported to Britain with great success. This particular example is in mahogany with a painted glass front panel. (Private collection)

32. This pair of candlesticks in the shape of dolphins is in pressed opaque blue and white glass. Probably made at Sandwich, U.S.A., it dates between 1840 and 1850. (The Metropolitan Museum of Art, New York, Bequest of Anna G. W. Green, in memory of Dr Charles W. Green)

33. Baseball, America's national sport, began to be played in the 1830s. It remained amateur till 1876, when the National League of Professional Baseball Clubs was established. In the same year, Isaac Broome of New Jersey made this baseball vase of parian ware for the Centennial Exhibition in Philadelphia. (The Brewer Collection of The New Jersey State Museum, Trenton)

33

of the Shakers, a religious sect based in New England 35 and New York. Their simple unadorned pieces have a special appeal to austere mid 20th-century taste.

Victorian silver both in England and America was influenced by the popular historical revivals, which meant that nothing escaped the need for ornament. 65,69 154 While the Victorians had every right to exercise their own tastes, it seems to me to have been an act of sacrilege to have plain Georgian teapots, sugar basins and 153 cream jugs embossed with endless streams of decoration, or to take the perfect line of a Georgian spoon and have it beaten into a flower-and-fruit encrusted berry spoon. The development of electroplating, like the 60,155 manufacture of pressed glass, brought silver into the homes of the masses. In ten years the pioneers of electroplate, the Birmingham firm of Elkington and Com- 40 pany, revolutionised the silver and plate trade, taking over completely from the Sheffield-plate industry.

British pottery and porcelain manufacture flourished and was very much in demand in America. From 5,6,43 the famous Staffordshire potteries came blue-and-white breakfast, dinner and tea services; from Copeland (formerly named Spode) came the well-known Italian 93 Landscape pattern; and various factories were producing the willow pattern, inspired by Chinese porcelain but originating in England towards the end of the 18th century. Coalport were manufacturing very ornate imitations of Sèvres, Dresden and Chelsea, sometimes even bearing copies of the original marks; but a lot of mid Victorian Coalport before 1881 bore no mark at all. Copeland was largely identified with parian ware, but also produced earthen- and chinawares, employing many fine artists to do the decorations like the German-born C. F. Hurten, well-known for his floral paintings. Although the main Derby factory closed in 1848, a group of potters moved to smaller premises where they carried on with many of the old traditional patterns and figures. A new company was formed in 1876 and from 1890 onwards was known as Royal Crown Derby. A new 43 departure from traditional work was made by Henry Doulton, who, after making various experiments in 25 decorated pottery, developed his new Art Pottery. Two notable artists whom he employed were George Tinworth and Hannah Barlow.

One of the most significant names in English pottery is that of Wedgwood, the firm started by the famous Josiah Wedgwood in the mid 18th century and still continuing in production today. During the 19th century many of their earlier wares were still being produced: jasperware medallions, busts in black basalt, and creamwares. During the Victorian era they also pro- 142 duced parian figures, biscuit barrels, cheese dishes, jugs, and plant pots, with and without the popular relief motifs. Most valuable of these items are the creamwares painted by Emile Lessore, which even in his own time 43 were treated as works of art.

The Minton factory was also producing work of good quality throughout the period, but there was a tendency to over decoration and ornateness. Much was influenced by the styles of Sèvres, but they also made

34. Advertisement for a Philadelphia furniture showroom. The top-heavy wardrobe, the elaborately carved piano, the deeply upholstered chairs and the whimsical lettering are typical of the popular taste of the time.

35. Shaker furniture. L. Brother's rocking chair and candle-stand. Absolute simplicity characterises the furniture of the American Shaker communities. (American Museum in Britain, Claverton Manor, Bath)

36. *Batchelor's Button,* a wallpaper designed by William Morris in 1892.

37. Dining-room sideboard in the 'Early English' style from *Hints on Household Taste* by Charles Lock Eastlake, first published in 1868.

35

21
80 parian and maiolica pieces, and the wonderful ceramics of M. L. Solon. Mason's ironstone was still being made, although under different patronage, and mention should be made of William de Morgan, friend of William Morris, for his decorated earthenware designs.

36,42 William Morris, Socialist, reformer, and craftsman, tried to raise the standard of popular taste in furniture, textiles, wallpapers and in what can best be termed a more aesthetic approach to life. He and his followers were in the main unsuccessful; the majority looked upon them as cranks who had dipped their sugared bread in the far too heady wine of Socialism.

In the main the new mood was for gilded, painted and decorated furniture. Mr William Morris and his disciples were to formulate their aesthetic creed, but their love of the past and belief that in this alone lay the hope for the future was like sowing seed on stony ground as far as the majority of wealthy people who could afford to support them were concerned. A few craftsmen were still making furniture that carried on the great legacy of cabinetmaking. They were trying to persuade people to support a higher standard in individual design and personal taste, but their pleas, like those of Morris, fell upon deaf ears. After all why make one piece of furniture by hand when the new machinery in the joiner's shop could turn out dozens of identical pieces in a shorter time? A fine veneer, a cleverly designed inlay, a touch of paint or gilt and these rather spurious examples of mass production were looked upon as the triumph of man's handiwork over his past slavery to time. The death of the craftsman and the rise of the industrialist were the symptoms and symbols of both the rise and fall of the Victorian era. The land, our home and heritage, was being neglected, in many cases forgotten, and in the smoke and grime of industrialism the seeds of two world wars and one major revolution that were to mar the 20th century were already being sown. A philosopher, living in comparative poverty, was already warning us that every economic system carries within itself the seeds of its own destruction. To the Britisher, who still saw the Union Jack as God's symbol on earth, Karl Marx's words sounded like arrant nonsense.

Let it not be thought that the age was completely negative. If it made the poor seem poorer it certainly made the newly rich richer, and it had many achievements that must stand to its credit. The inventions of Faraday and Bell; the introduction of the postal
61 service; the magnificent accomplishments of Brunel; the rise of The Cunard Steamship Company, followed rapidly by its competitors; increase in foreign travel; new openings for thousands of emigrants; all these things must be noted, but they all in one way or another spelt one word, and that was 'money'.

Victoriana, a word to dream about and conjure with, was a phase of the past that we are now beginning to see as the promise of the future. Its furniture, bric-à-brac, paintings, silver and ceramics are today taking on a new lease of life. Indeed, we might well echo the phrase, 'The Queen is dead, long live the Queen'.

36

37

38

39

38

40

41

38. Fine walnut loo or breakfast table with carved tripod pedestal base. Designed and made by Henry Palmer of Bath, 1849. (Victoria and Albert Museum, London)

39. Water jug and two goblets with intaglio cut decoration. Probably Stourbridge, 1850–1853. Stourbridge was the home of traditional heavily cut lead glass, but with the increased demand for cheaper domestic glass, manufacturers looked for more modest ways of using the metal. (Victoria and Albert Museum, London)

40. Electroplated card case by Elkington and Company. The use of an electric current to give a silver or gold skin to a base-metal object was pioneered by Elkington's of Birmingham and met with instant success, in spite of a hostile rearguard action from the doomed Sheffield plate industry. (Private collection)

41. Jug with relief pattern of blossom. Made by Pinder, Bourne and Company, of Burslem, England. The design, which was first registered in 1877, shows the influence of Japanese art. (Victoria and Albert Museum, London)

42. Group of chairs showing trends in English Victorian furniture design.

1-4 show four historical revivals: so-called Classical, Medieval, Elizabethan and Louis XV.

1. Carved mahogany dining chair in the Grecian style, designed by Philip Hardwick in 1834 and made by W. and C. Wilkinson.
(Worshipful Company of Goldsmiths, London)
2. Carved oak armchair in the Medieval style, designed by A. W. N. Pugin and made by J. G. Grace for Scarisbrook Hall, Lancashire, c. 1840.
(Victoria and Albert Museum, London)
3. Carved mahogany chair in the Elizabethan style, upholstered with tent-stitch embroidery, c. 1845.
(Victoria and Albert Museum, London)
4. Mid Victorian walnut chair with upholstered back and metal mounts in the style of Louis XV.
(Private collection)

5-7 Three popular designs.

5. Adaptation of the balloon-back. Walnut, with upholstered panel in the back, c. 1860.
(Private collection)
6. The classic balloon-back. Mahogany dining chair with upholstered seat, made by G. M. and H. J. Storey of London Wall.
7. Oak dining chair upholstered in leather. Designed by T. C. Collcutt and made by Collinson and Lock, c. 1872.
(Victoria and Albert Museum, London)

8-9 Two extremes.

8. Papier-mâché chair with rush seat, painted decoration and inlaid with mother of pearl, c. 1860. (Victoria and Albert Museum, London)

9. Solid oak hall chair made for Osborne House, Isle of Wight. Hall chairs were traditionally made in solid wood so that the wet clothes of the messengers and servants who used them would not spoil precious upholstery.

10-12 Three chairs by experimental designers.

10. Sussex chair of ebonised beech with a rush seat. Made by Morris and Company from c. 1865. (Victoria and Albert Museum, London)

11. Ash ladder-back chair with rush seat. Designed and made by Ernest Gimson. c. 1888. (Victoria and Albert Museum, London).

12. Art-Nouveau style chair designed by Charles Rennie Mackintosh, c. 1897. (Victoria and Albert Museum, London)

1

43. Group of plates.

1. Strawberry design 'Belleek' type plate by Ott and Brewer of Trenton, New Jersey. 1880s.
(Newark Museum, Newark, New Jersey)
2. Coalport china dish with typical floral bouquet.
(Private collection)
3. Wedgwood plate with design by the outstanding figure painter Emile Lessore.
(Victoria and Albert Museum, London)

4. Stone china Minton plate
with transfer-printed design
in underglaze blue. Passion
flower pattern. 1850.
(Victoria and Albert
Museum, London)

5. Royal Crown Derby plate
with G and M monogram.
Made to celebrate the
marriage of Princess Mary
of Teck and the Duke of
York (later George V). 1893.

THE VICTORIAN HOUSE

SOLID and foursquare, the Victorian house represented to the Victorians all their hopes and achievements. Even when we speak of the house we are faced with the rise of a many-tiered system of dwelling places. Let us look first at the homes of the upper middle classes. These were the merchants, bankers and younger sons of the gentry who were prepared to soil their hands and weaken their social position by becoming involved in trade. Their houses were either the town-houses of the older families who had sold them as they saw the grinding wheels of industry approaching and threatening their elegant way of life, or houses they commissioned for themselves and had built by architects who were prepared to be their slaves rather than their masters. Whereas the 18th-century gentleman would commission a house and leave it to the architect and builder once he had approved the plans; the Victorian would want it built largely to his own specifications. This often meant that a house was badly designed and out of proportion, with only one criterion as to its worthiness and that was what it had cost to build.

Let us now examine a typical residence of one of these upper middle-class families. It has been built in the outskirts of the town in wooded grassland so that the garden can be disguised to resemble a small park. The building itself is of red brick and is shaped like a foreshortened E, the height out of proportion with the attic rooms in order to house the domestics. A heavy stone arch with recumbent lions at its base marks the entrance. Just inside is a small cottage for the gardener or coachman which the owner hopes will suggest a guarded lodge to deter intruders. The front of the house has large windows in Gothic surrounds downstairs, while upstairs they are of a more conventional oblong shape. Once the visitor's eye has swept along the frontal with its imposing doorway and ornate windows it

would not deign to look up. A cobbled path leads to the paved stable yard with loose-boxes on one side and coach-house on the other. At the end is the harness room and in it the polished leather harnesses with their gleaming brass fittings (silver-plated fittings might well be used on the family carriage). Hanging on the wall is a collection of horse brasses all gleaming with the pure gold of the midday sun.

In the coach-house standing in pride of place is the family carriage, a large, ornate affair capable of using two or even four horses and of carrying papa, mama, the nurse or governess and all the family. Then there is the brougham, a vehicle of swan-like grace used mainly by the ladies when making calls; a gig, the pride of father as he trotted round the neighbourhood raising his hat to passers-by as much to draw attention to himself as to pay them his respects; a governess cart for children's outings; a tub for when mother went on social journeys into the village or town; and, of course, the inevitable wagonette, used mainly for picnics on summer days. The stables contain from two to four horses and a pony, and there, in a loose-box especially constructed for its accommodation, is the trotting pony.

Let us now go into the house itself. A large entrance hall leads on one side to the drawing room and opposite it to the dining room. Beyond is the study or library and the room mainly hallowed for the use of the womenfolk, the sitting room, the name of which tells us exactly what it was, the room to which the ladies retired when they had nothing else to do or nowhere else to go. Beyond the study there might well be a second reception room leading into the conservatory and then into the garden.

On the other side at the back is a large kitchen with its double oven and huge fireplace, and a scullery,

44. An ornate but practical washstand designed by William Burges for his London house. The top part is a water tank inset with small mirrors, the fittings are bronze, and the bowl and its surround are marble.
(Victoria and Albert Museum, London)

on the shelves of which stand the innumerable pans essential to the culinary arts. (It was a period, let us remember, when Samuel Smiles frowned on every member of the household, and if Satan was to find work for idle hands those idle hands were not to be found in the kitchen.) A stone passage leads from the kitchen into the stable yard, on one side of which is the larder and on the other the laundry. The larder faces north to take advantage of the cold, and to aid this there are ventilating bricks let into the walls and marble slabs around the back and on each side. A stairway from the passage leads down to the coal cellars and it is in these that the younger members of the family might find themselves locked up as punishment if they break the strict moral code laid down by their father.

The main staircase, a trifle too heavy and ornate for the entrance hall, sweeps up to the first floor, dividing at the top into two passages leading to the landings and then to the bedrooms. The two large front bedrooms are used by the parents and sundry visitors; the rooms at the back are for the children and also include a nursery and a bathchamber. In the bathchamber is a large iron and enamelled bath encased in wooden walls, a smaller hip bath, a foot bath and a tub for the children. A marble washstand stands in the corner. A wooden table with a marble top holds a large bowl and soap dish. All the water, both hot and cold, has to be carried up in pails by the servants and likewise emptied. For this, copper ladling cans are used which enable the last drops of dirty water to be scooped up. Later the water will be heated by a large boiler that stands in one corner; it has to be lit each night to provide hot water for the morning. There might also be one of the fashionable steam-bath cabinets that preceded the turkish bath, and perhaps a portable shower; this went under the unlikely name of a pneumatic bath.

45. Pottery plaques with inscriptions, religious or sentimental, were best-sellers in mid Victorian times, just as prints of tearful children or Chinese girls are today. This plaque, with its painted frame, is Sunderland ware. (Private collection)

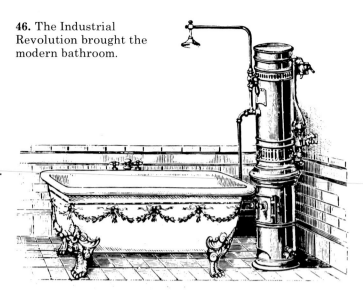

46. The Industrial Revolution brought the modern bathroom.

Having looked at the house, let us turn to its occupants. There is father, mother and offspring: a child every eighteen months is commonplace. A housekeeper, butler-valet, lady's maid, parlourmaid, housemaid, nursemaid, cook and kitchenmaid make up the inside staff. Outside there is the gardener and his boys, the groom and his stable-lad, the coachman and his assistant. There is also a governess, too grand to be grouped with the servants below stairs; she is a lonely outcast marooned on the island of her own self importance.

The next group of houses is smaller than the one we have described, either detached or semi-detached but conforming to its outline in most details. Then there are the terraces of lower middle-class homes, lived in by artisans, small shopkeepers and craftsmen. Finally, there are the long dreary rows of back-to-backs where the labouring classes live out their miserable existence. The average middle-class Victorian had a callous attitude to suffering. If the poor starved in the workhouse they had not been prudent enough, and if the rich ended in bankruptcy they had been far too reckless. Money was their God and they used it to pay their way in this world for six days of the week, and to put enough on the collection plate on the seventh to assure themselves of a comfortable place in the hereafter.

These then were the houses of the people who formed the backbone of the Victorian age. On the surface the Victorians were conformists, followers of the Established Church. It is true there were some who called themselves Nonconformists, who elevated their exact idea of Christian ethics to the level of what they were pleased to look upon as a social conscience. But what mattered to them all, above everything else both in life and in death, were their possessions. From the cradle to the grave, possessions dominated their whole lives, as their ornately carved cradles and their heavily brassed and ornamented coffins are witness.

These were the people whose outlook was to be immortalised by the incorrigible Oscar Wilde when he said they knew 'the price of everything and the value of nothing'. These were the people whose passion for

47

47. American side chair of hickory and maple with turned legs and stretchers, a rush seat and gilt stencilled decoration on black paint. These cheap 'fancy' chairs were popularised in the 1830s by Lambert Hitchcock of Connecticut and chairs of this type were found in many American homes. (Private collection)

48. This chandelier of about 1840 supports six oil lamps of the type named after the Swiss inventor Argand, who first produced them in the 1780s. They used a cylindrical wick so that they burned with a brighter flame. (Victoria and Albert Museum, London)

49. One of the objectives of the International Association of Working Men was the eight-hour working day, and this watch case is believed to be one of twelve made in the 1860s to mark the meeting of the Association in London. (Trades Union Congress, London)

ornamentation drove them to beat effusive designs on priceless gold plate and to ruin Georgian silver with superfluous embossed patterns. A few men of culture **153** and taste tried to tell them their mistakes. 'Cranks and humbugs' was the reply, and yet another monstrosity was added to their collection of curiosities, a pottery plaque with a text, perhaps, warning, 'Thou God seest **45** me', or, over the housemaid's bed, the more appropriate warning, 'Be prepared for ye know not at what hour the master cometh'.

The Victorians were, in the main, tasteless vulgarians, and it is their possessions we shall be looking at in the rest of these pages. Room by room we shall take a glimpse at them and at what they valued. All and nothing will be the final answer.

48

49

50. A surrey, complete with its 'fringe on top'.

51. This carriage, or 'Pilentum', was made by 'Mr Mulliner of Northampton' and exhibited at the Great Exhibition of 1851. The canework is imitation and is painted 'so successfully as almost to deceive the eye'. Indeed, elegant though the actual carriage undoubtedly must have been, one cannot help feeling that the delicate grace, particularly of the wheels and springs, owes much to the skill of the advertising artist.

52. Horse brasses for decorating harness have an honourable history dating back to Biblical times. These are traditional designs: decorated crosses, three moons, a large heart surrounded by a number of smaller ones, and a sun.

53. Hearse. A middle-class funeral was a festive occasion.

54. This huge brass watch (reproduced actual size) has various names–coach clock, chaise clock, Goliath clock. It was made to be carried in a pocket of a coach or to hang on a hook during a journey. (Private collection) The wallpaper is an Owen Jones design of the 1840s.

50

51

52

53

54

56. Cradle of carved oak, painted and gilded, by Norman Shaw. Shaw was a well-known London architect (he built the Gaiety Theatre) and he and his followers were so impressed by William Morris's designs that they took to designing furniture themselves. The spirit of Morris's Arts and Crafts Movement and of his reaction against Victorian bad taste is clear in this charming cradle, with its feeling for the material and the innocent delight in the decoration—the signs of the Zodiac, the flowers and birds and the final enchanting touch of the stars painted inside the canopy.
(Victoria and Albert Museum, London)

57. Dolls' house. The domestic dramas of Victorian life were acted out in miniature within these walls.
(Private collection)

55. *A Home on the Mississippi*. Lithograph by Currier and Ives, the most prolific American lithographic printing firm of the 19th century.
(Private collection)

56

A HOME ON THE MISSISSIPPI.

55

THE HALL & STAIRCASE

AVING briefly glanced at a typical upper middle-class residence, let us now take a closer look, room by room. Outward appearances were an all-important factor in the Victorian house. The first thing the eye alights on when the door is opened is the entrance hall with its imposing staircase. The visitor must be assured at first glance that this is the home of a well-to-do family, one that will leave its mark on the town. Here in 1840 there might be a carefully executed reproduction of a Tudor court cupboard, a heavily carved oak closet for hats and coats, an oblong oak table with a silver salver for visiting cards, probably a fine 18th-century barometer hanging on the wall, and, standing at the end of the hallway, a longcase clock–called a grandfather clock by the Victorians–its loud tick and clear chimes dominating everything else.

Later the oak will be replaced by mahogany, the closet by a hall-stand with a mirror and hooks, and an oval console table will replace its rectangular counterpart. The court cupboard will disappear and where it had stood will be a small decorative table flanked by two matching hall chairs. The design of the table might have been inspired by Sheraton and the chairs influenced by Chippendale but if either of these gentlemen were to have returned they would have haunted the occupants for taking monstrous liberties with their original ideas.

What spoils so much of this furniture, that today makes it look crude to the critical eye? The answer is quite simple: heaviness. The carving was often crude, the legs too thick and the stretchers too clumsy. Size rather than quality determined value and significance. The story is told of an industrial magnate who asked how many chairs there should be in a dining room suite and was told ten diners and two carvers to which he replied, 'Well, make mine with twenty diners and four carvers; that will make some of the neighbours sit up!'.

In 1840 the walls of the hall are either panelled or painted. A weighty brass oil lamp stands on the table. **58** This has to be trimmed and filled each morning, and is lit as dusk falls each evening to cast a soft glow over the darkened hall. Standing beside the staircase is a palm in a colourful pottery jardinière and a marble figure on **108** a black plinth.

But let us move on upstairs. The grand staircase might be of stone, marble or wood and is carpeted, with a banister of plain mahogany. The stairs divide at the top to form twin galleries overlooking the hall. At the head of the stairs there is another longcase clock, made by a local clockmaker and bearing his name and date of manufacture on its face. Over the clock is a large oil painting, again the work of a local artist. These oil paintings were so commonplace that today most of them are not worth the cost of canvas and oils, let alone the ornate gilt frames in which they are mounted.

Twenty years later the walls will be hung with prints showing the march of progress, like *Travelling on the Liverpool and Manchester Railway*, printed and published by Raphael Tuck and Sons, a firm which also did much to popularise another novelty, the picture postcard. There might be an engraving of the *Great Britain*, the first large iron steamship to use the screw **61** propeller, and the gigantic *Great Eastern*. They are a **29** tribute to the designer, Brunel, the engineering genius whose ribbon-like steel bridges span the Menai Straits and the Avon at Clifton, whose Great Western Railway has crossed chasms and burrowed through mountains.

A blanket chest and linen coffer stands on one of the side landings, and outside the door of the main bedroom there is a small table on which the maid can stand the breakfast trays. At the end of the landing a narrow staircase leads to the attics.

58. Typical oil lamp with an engraved glass shade.

59. Yorkshire longcase clock by Smith of Wrexham. Yorkshire longcase clocks were produced when the Industrial Revolution began to bring prosperity to the north of England. Their main characteristic is their size: they are gigantic. (Private collection)

58

59

60. Electroplated tray. The rim is decorated in the Renaissance style from a model by the sculptor and designer Alfred Stevens. By Thomas Bradbury and Sons, Sheffield, 1856. (Victoria and Albert Museum, London)

61. The *Great Britain* on her maiden voyage. The first propeller-driven iron steamship was designed by I. K. Brunel and built in 1843. The full complement of sail was a precaution insisted on by faint-hearted traditionalists who did not trust the new method of propulsion. The ship was recently towed from the Falkland Islands to Bristol and will become a floating museum.

62. In 1884, when Charles Tisch of New York made this elaborate rosewood cabinet, collecting knick-knacks – porcelain, curiosities, souvenirs – was all the rage. Of bolder design than its English prototypes, this cabinet's asymmetrical compartments were, no doubt, designed to take articles of various sizes and shapes. Little is known about Tisch. He is listed in directories between 1870 and 1889 in turn as carver, cabinetmaker and a dealer in 'art' furniture. In 1889 he offered this cabinet as a gift to the Metropolitan Museum, stating: 'This piece of Furniture received the first price *(sic)* at the New Orleans Exposition 84/85. It is a purely American production of my own Manufacture and consider it worthy of a place in the Museum.' (The Metropolitan Museum of Art, New York, Gift of Charles Tisch)

60

61

The Dining Room

ET us now return to the ground floor and move into the dining room. This is in some ways the most important room in the house, for, if we can believe Miss Eliza Acton and Mrs Beeton, a Victorian's heart lay very close to his stomach. Here the servants work all morning polishing the furniture and silver and seeing that all is in order for the first main meal of the day, luncheon. Tea will be served on small tables in the sitting room and this is mainly a feminine gathering, but at about six the dining room will be made ready again for the second gargantuan feast. After dinner the gentlemen will remain to drink their port and smoke cigars, telling their racy stories or talking over their business deals, while the ladies retire to the drawing room to hear all that is going on in the town and to smile sedately over the mishaps of their neighbours.

The oak dining table is large and oval with a centre leaf that can be removed. The chairs are the **42** mahogany balloon-back type which, with variations, remained popular from the 1830s to the late 1860s. A serving table stands to one side, but the room is domin- **20** ated by the enormous mahogany sideboard. (Some Victorian sideboards were curved and bow fronted in such an exaggerated fashion that they appeared to be in a permanent state of pregnancy.) There are drawers for cutlery and wine coasters, cupboards for glasses of all **64** shapes and sizes and a cellaret, a cupboard fitted with racks to store wine in. It is part of the butler's work to supervise the sideboard and its contents. In another drawer of the sideboard is the table linen, large cloths of pure Irish linen or patterned damask with matching napkins, all hand laundered to a whiteness that would make the detergent lovers of today green with envy.

On top of the sideboard is a silver tea and coffee **69** service, and at each end are two huge vases from one of the European factories.

A small cupboard with a marble top and a brass gallery stands alongside the sideboard. In this are kept bottles of port, sherry, madeira, whisky and brandy and these will be used to refill the decanters of the tantalus **70** which stands on top.

A large silver and cut-glass cruet stands in the **63** centre of the table, and at each end are five-stemmed candlesticks, for, although an oil lamp hangs over the **48** table, the evening meal will be taken by candlelight. **65**

You may be surprised to learn that in most Victorian dining rooms there were one or two spittoons discreetly tucked away in corners and brought out for use when the ladies had retired. These were made of carved wood, heavy pottery or decorated brass; the glass lining, which was half filled with sand or sawdust, was emptied and washed out each evening.

Victorian dining-room silver and cutlery is becoming very much sought after today. One reason for this is the weight of silver each piece contains; another is the fact that Georgian silver is becoming so rare and has almost priced itself out of the market. Each generation expresses its personality through its possessions and the Victorians saw silver as an open sesame to the social world which they longed to inhabit.

The one good thing we can say about the silver of this period is that it was still being made, or its manufacture was supervised, by master craftsmen. They would take a simple shape, put on it a slightly heavier handle, then decorate it with a few curves and flourishes to make it acceptable to their dictatorial masters. Wine coasters no longer have the simple turned rim, dotted with tiny studs to give a point of emphasis; now the rim has been thickened and decorated with ribbons, garlands of flowers or bunches of grapes, even the heads of birds and beasts. Sets of salts, these usually consisted of four matching pieces, were treated in the same manner. Simpler, pierced pieces, peppers, salts, mustards, sugar

63. Silver cruet with eight cut-glass bottles. Maker's mark C.F. Sheffield, 1868.

64. Group of typical plain, cut and engraved Victorian drinking glasses in common use in most middle-class homes. (Private collection)

65. Place setting. American sterling silver cutlery and silver-plated candelabrum set off to perfection the Limoges porcelain and cut glass in this elegant place setting for a Victorian gentleman of taste. (Private collection)

66. Brownfield dinner plate. (Private collection)

67. Colour-printed plate by F. and R. Pratt of Fenton, *c.* 1850. (Victoria and Albert Museum, London)

68. Cranberry glass. Victorian red glass was found in shades of ruby, cranberry and pink. (Private collection)

66

67

68

basins and bon-bon dishes, each with its blue glass lining, were to appear towards the end of the period.

In the glass cupboard in pride of place is a set of Venetian goblets in deep ruby decorated with white and coloured enamels, carefully gilded to emphasise the design. There are also wine glasses of various sizes in amber, red, green or blue, and a complete suite of Waterford crystal. Cut glass of all types was very dear to their hearts for its cleanly cut grooves and angles flashed out all the prismatic colours of the rainbow and gave them an inner satisfaction as they thought, 'this is the best that money can buy'.

The dinner service itself is probably in Wedgwood, Minton or Coalport. Many of their designs were simple, for these potteries were still very much influenced by the Chinese and Dutch patterns that were brought to England at the time of William and Mary, and blue-and-white ware was extremely popular. But in the middle years of the Victorian age the more elaborate designs of Derby, Chelsea and Worcester became fashionable.

One or two prints or steel engravings decorate the panelled walls, and there, over the fireplace, is the portrait of father, painted by an artist who was well-known for his family portraits in oils. This is no Rembrandt or Gainsborough; its pride of place is entirely due to its subject matter and fifty years on it might well find its way to the attics or a local junk shop.

In the same dining room some forty years later the panelling will have disappeared and in its place will be one of the fashionable wallpapers. The massive sideboard will have given way to a more elegant piece of furniture, a cross between a chiffonier and a Welsh dresser, and the side tables will be serpentine fronted. The chairs will resemble those of Adam, Sheraton or Chippendale. The spittoons will have been thrown away or taken to the attic to be forgotten. The silver cutlery will be simpler and more elegant, and the glassware will likewise reflect the new trend towards simplicity, perhaps influenced by William Morris and his followers in the Arts and Crafts Movement. The candlesticks remain, but the hanging oil lamp will have been dispensed with and in its place will be a gasolier, a gaslit chandelier with coloured glass smoke domes that can be taken down and washed as occasion demands. The dining table will be of the long D-end type, made of mahogany, walnut or even rosewood instead of the heavy oak of the earlier period. These changes all bore witness to the social revolution which had taken place among the merchants and industrialists of the day. Their money had bought them a place in society and from their new way of life they were learning something of taste and the social graces.

If I have left the dining room somewhat sparse and bare it is because that is how we would have found it. Later generations might embellish it with plaques, pictures, wall-brackets and all the paraphernalia that was to become part of the Edwardian scene. To the Victorians the church was the temple of the soul and the dining room the temple of the stomach.

69. Silver tea and coffee set with Classical design, 1872. (Victoria and Albert Museum, London)

70. 'Tantalus' with three cut-glass spirit decanters. The alternate-panel pattern on a square decanter was the most popular Victorian design. The excellent quality of the cutting on these pieces shows that fine craftsmanship still flourished in spite of the demand for cheap mass-produced goods. The brass-bound case and lock are typical of the period. (Author's collection)

71. Mahogany chiffonier, c. 1850. A chiffonier was often used as a sideboard in the morning room. They were very fashionable in the early and mid Victorian periods. The simple lines allow the grain of the wood to be seen to the best advantage. (Collection Mrs G. M. Gloag)

69

70

71

The Drawing Room

HE year is 1847. The house seems to have changed: it is lighter, and even papa appears to be filled with a sense of liveliness and joie de vivre. The Queen is happily married and well-bedded and her Prince Consort seems to be the fairy prince of every girl's dream. The dining room was, as we have seen, very much, the domain of the paterfamilias. The drawing room was shared since it was used in the morning for mother to receive her guests and in the evening by the family to retire to after dinner. Therefore it must have a touch of feminine charm as well as an emphasis of masculine superiority. It was the withdrawing room, hence its name. The word lounge would have been an anathema to the Victorians, suggesting the worst vice of all, laziness.

In many ways it is the most attractive room in
73 the house. Its main furnishings are a large settee, or sofa, daintily painted chairs around the walls and several occasional tables. On the walls are brackets,
21 and on these stand vases and figures by Meissen, Min-
77 ton and Samson of Paris. The Oriental mood, so dear to the heart of the Prince Regent in an earlier reign, still holds its place and can be seen in a cleverly disguised reproduction or a piece of Chinese porcelain.

On the chimney piece is a massive clock flanked
80 by vases. It might be Viennese, German or Italian. Capodimonte was already in favour and plant pots from this famous Italian factory were becoming popular. A boulle display cabinet stands against the far wall, a copy of an 18th-century design. In it are the valuable pieces of porcelain, many brought by papa and his business friends from their trips to Europe; others are gifts from foreign traders. This was the age of expansion and all Europe, the near and Far East were seeking to court Victorian affluence.

The fine knotted-pile carpet is from the Axminster looms, recently taken over by Wilton, and there are also several Persian rugs as well. The walls are newly covered with an expensive hand-printed wallpaper by Owen Jones, and hanging from the centre 54 of the ceiling is a large crystal chandelier. In the corner, standing casually as though it was meant to be unnoticed but was determined to be seen, is an upright grand by Collards. A music stool and lattice music cabinet stand nearby. In the bay windows is a display of pot plants, in elaborate wire jardinières and in pots on tall stands. The pots themselves are in many cases more colourful than the plants they contain. In front of the fireplace is a heavy brass fender and firedogs to support the poker, tongs and shovel. To one side stands a coal bucket, the lid discreetly closed and enhanced by a bold and heavy patterning. The overmantel could never pass unnoticed; it is a large, ornate, gilded and garlanded mirror that reflects all the contents of the room and also enables a lady to adjust her hat before returning to her waiting carriage after a morning call.

The mistress of the house and her daughters are diligent needlewomen and the sofa, chairs and firescreen are covered by designs in petit-point and grosspoint embroideries. These were worked on trammed canvasses that were already being imported from the Viennese factories. On the walls are engravings and one or two nondescript water-colours. Many of these tell a story or focus on a moral like *Little Lady Bountiful*, a pathetic scene depicting a woodland picnic at which the youngest child distributes the debris of a feast to poor children who stand discreetly by.

The marriage of Victoria to Prince Albert gave everything Germanic a special place in the Court and hence this was reflected in the furniture and furnishings

72. This elegant rosewood armchair is one of a pair from a sitting-room of a house at 816 Broad Street, Meriden, Connecticut, and was part of a suite of Renaissance revival furnishings. The house, which was completed in 1870, was built for Jedediah Wilcox, a wealthy carpetbag manufacturer. (The Metropolitan Museum of Art, New York, Gift of Josephine M. Fiala)

73. Two well-upholstered sofas illustrated in Storey's 1865 catalogue of furniture designs.

74. 'Writing table in the French Style'. From *Furniture and Decoration, 1892*. The writer says, 'The Louis Quinze desk . . . which we publish herewith, though it may miss much of the charm that invests . . . old cabinet work, at the same time lacks much of the costliness, for it has been designed with a view to being useful to those who manufacture for the middle-class trade.'

of the rising middle classes. Later, French influence was also felt. Although Waterloo had been fought in 1815 and the British still viewed the French with a certain amount of suspicion, at the time of the Second Empire, French furniture became very fashionable and painted and gilded tables, cabinets and chairs were to become **78** a feature of the drawing rooms of this period.

Let us glance for a moment into the drawing room on a morning in the early summer of 1847. In the **75** room are three or four ladies being entertained by the mistress of the house. She is hatless and is wearing a soft, lilac moire dress sweeping to the floor with frills and furbelows, while at her neck is a dainty Brussels lace fichu. Her earrings are simple gold pendants and on her hands she wears several rings, all encrusted with precious stones set in heavy claws which were so fashionable then. Her guests are all wearing hats. Their dresses are long, sweeping graciously behind them and giving the suggestion of a train. Some are in satin, others in flowered voiles, but the most striking is in flower-encrusted silk from Lyons. This is one of the daily fashion parades that form an essential part of Victorian life. They are sitting, holding small Bristol glasses in the popular claret shade, sipping their madeira as they chatter about the many trivialities that fill their humdrum lives.

On their shapely arms they wear heavy gold bangles with tiny locks that suggest their proper roles, feminine slaves in the Victorian marriage market. Some of the pendants are French made, semi-precious stones set in elaborate gold settings. One wears a locket with a painted miniature of the child she has lost on one side and a lock of its hair on the other. Hair jewel- **76** lery was often worn and hair is found twisted with gold wires into bracelets, or mounted in heavy oval frames for brooches, or even stranded and inlaid into gold bands for rings. These tokens of their loved and departed ones were very dear to the hearts of the Victorians. With death came also the appropriate jewellery. **76** The emeralds, sapphires and diamonds were stored away for at least six months, and in their place black jet necklaces and earrings would be worn, black-edged pendants with a picture of the dear departed inset behind a glass front, and black runs on which are found one or two tiny pearls, the symbol of tears.

On this particular day the mistress is showing her latest toy, a small decorative scent bottle and vinaigrette combined, and a novelty her husband has **81** just bought himself, a shoe snuff-box. At eleven thirty **83** the carriages are called and the ladies prepare to leave, each carrying a parasol, some of silk and lace, others of satin and beads, some with cane handles, others of bone and ivory. The sun is now just starting to stream into the room so the latest innovation, the Venetian blinds, are dropped to prevent its merciless rays from fading the colours of the curtains and needlework. The pelmet hangs like a heavy festoon and the curtains are swept back and held in position by chased brass bands. As the last visitor leaves, the mistress moves towards her sitting room to work at her embroidery until luncheon. **116**

75.
In the 1840s French fashion plates broke away from the tradition of the
single posed figure and introduced informal groups against everyday backgrounds.
The popularity of these charming plates soon spread to England where they
remained a feature of ladies' journals for many years.

76. Victorian jewellery: cabochon garnets, cameos, mourning jet, hair and hearts all played their part.

THE RIGHT WAY

77. Pair of mugs decorated in the style of 18th-century Worcester by Samson of Paris. (Private collection)

78. A rosewood cabinet by Roux of New York with Sèvres plaques in the Renaissance revival style, 1866. (The Metropolitan Museum of Art, New York, Edgar J. Kaufmann Charitable Foundation Fund)

79. Inexpensive Victorian jewellery. On the left, Italian mosaic brooch and studs on ebony bases. On the right, right, filigree gold and turquoise brooch and earrings. (Private collection)

80. Minton pâte-sur-pâte clock garniture by the supreme master of this extremely delicate 'paste upon paste' method of ceramic decoration, Marc Louis Solon, 1871.

77

78

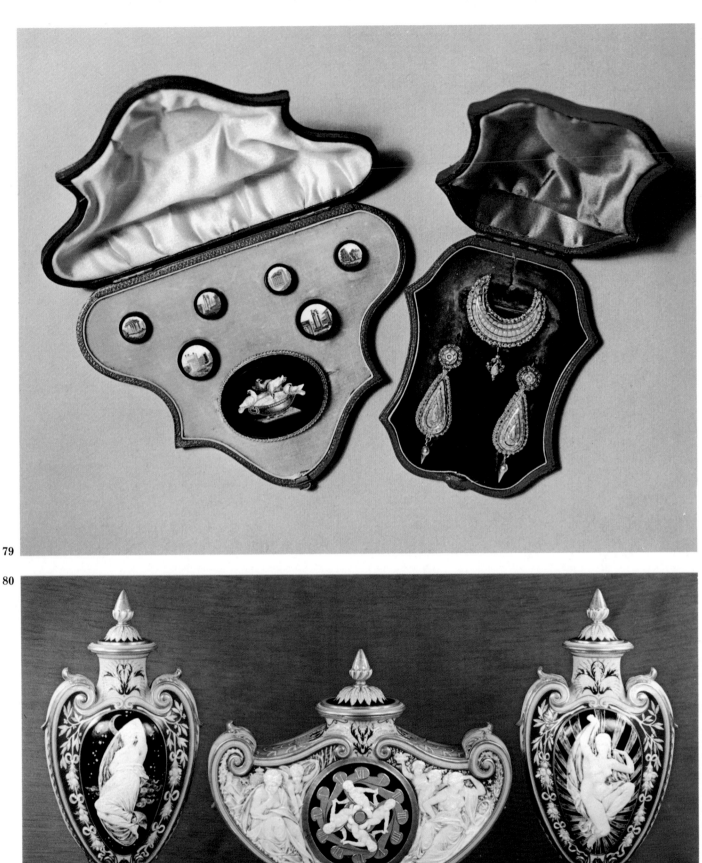

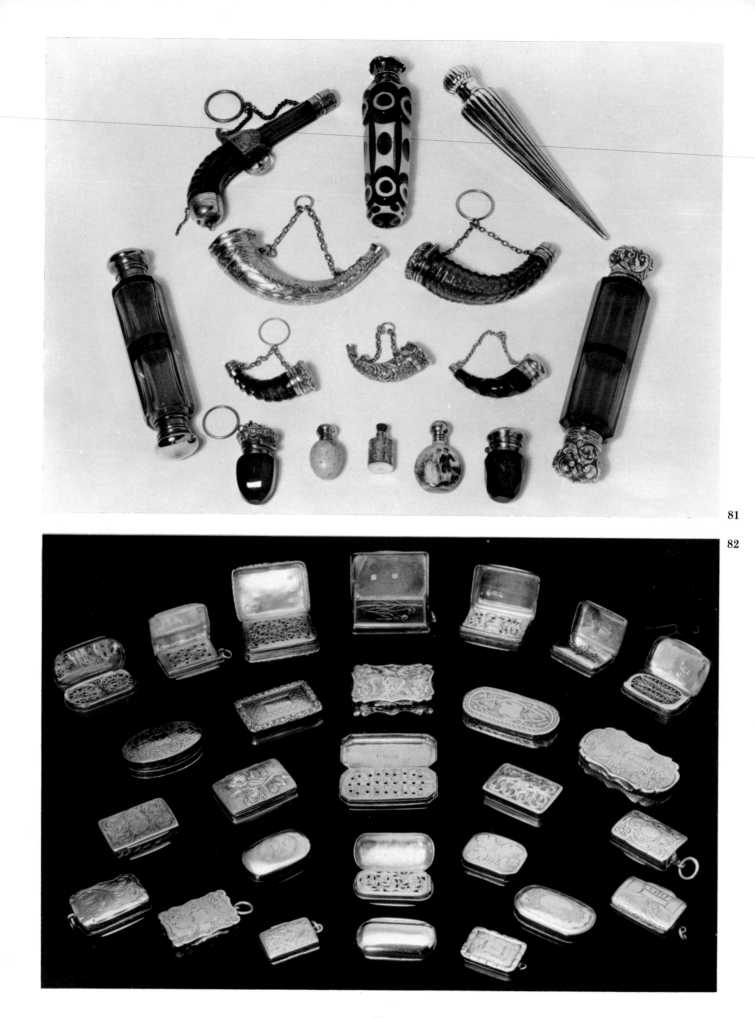

81. Group of scent bottles in silver and coloured glass. Some are combined with vinaigrettes. (Private collection)

82. Group of English vinaigrettes. These exquisite boxes contained smelling salts to revive a delicate constitution. The boxes with the punched holes are less interesting than those with the filigree. (Private collection)

83. An interesting group of shoe snuff-boxes for a collector of unusual items. (Private collection)

83

THE SITTING ROOM

EHIND the drawing room is the sitting room. This is an entirely feminine domain and is the most elaborately furnished and cluttered room in the house. Here the ladies of the house indulge in embroidery or water-colour painting and waste their time in idle gossip.

The curtains are embroidered linen and a long lace curtain hangs across the window to shield the occupants from prying eyes. The walls are papered with one of the fashionable sprig designs and on the floor is a new Wilton moquette carpet, picking up the pastel shades of the paintwork.

On the walls are plaques, some from abroad, others made at Leeds and later at Doulton. There too is 90 a sampler that the mistress had worked with her own hands in her own days in the schoolroom. Ornate picture 84 frames contain oils, prints, and water-colours of birds and flowers. There are also silhouettes and some of 89 Stevens' charming woven-silk pictures.

The sitting room is mainly used in the afternoons. Here the tea-drinking ritual, comparatively new to the English home, takes place with all the elaborate ceremony of the same event in the palace of a Chinese mandarin. Tea might even be served in tiny cups from China, but more often in teaware from Rockingham, Worcester 93 or Spode. This then is the fine and private place of the Victorian woman, for an hour or two she can escape from her endless round of domestic duties, social calls and good works, and live, at least in her imagination, her own life.

The fireplace is small and inlaid with marble with a matching marble mantel-shelf. On the mantel-shelf is a clock flanked by matching ornaments. Most of these clocks were European in origin and were often set on onyx or marble bases with a gilt figure on top and two matching figures on pedestals at each side; or the casing might be of porcelain and beautifully painted by

hand with flowers or birds or scrolls or shields. The faces of many of these clocks were heavily enamelled and on some the hours were marked out in semi-precious stones. These things were very lovely in themselves, but, alas, much of their beauty was lost in the overcrowded room.

On each side of the fireplace are fitted shelves in arched alcoves with wall sconces in white wood, gilded plaster or brass. On the shelves in the alcoves are vases from Delft in the delicate blue-and-white ware that had been copied from the Chinese (delftware was also made in England), lovely figures from Vienna reflecting the arrogant and courtly characters of that city, Dresden figures and Staffordshire pottery of the best period by 140 Ralph or Enoch Wood. There is a Wedgwood Greek urn, and Worcester and Derby vases that are equal to those of their European rivals. For the liberal Nonconformists, who played an important part in Victorian life, there are busts of Wesley and Spurgeon, but favourite of all and found in every household are figures of the Queen and her Consort.

The oil lamps are of glass and porcelain, decor- 58 ated or overlaid, but with a charm and delicacy that appeals to a feminine heart. The chairs in the room are small and again delicate, some with upholstered seats in golden damask or flowered brocade. Some are gilded, others painted, and some varnished; hence cheaper 47 woods like pine were being used. Small tables are scattered everywhere, rosewood, satinwood and walnut painted with rural scenes, or inlaid with designs of fruit, flowers or musical instruments. There is also a papier-mâché table and on it a papier-mâché tray and 87 letter rack. Papier mâché had been popular for small

84. Fireside corner in a sitting room. On the mantelpiece: cross-stitch face screens, plates, pots and commemorative mug. On the wall: paintings, prints and photographs in ornate frames. On the table: oil lamp with windmill, ivory-bound books, mother-of-pearl lady's companion, spun-glass birds in a dome, bead-work 'miser' purse and ruby-glass vase. On the floor: a decorated coal-scuttle.

decorative items such as boxes and trays, gilded and inlaid with mother-of-pearl, and later even items of furniture were made in it, tables, chairs and even beds.

One thing that must be said about the Victorian ladies is that they were born magpies. They collected and they accumulated possessions until every table and shelf in the sitting room was groaning with pottery, porcelain and glass. So we find in the corner the inevitable whatnot. Sometimes it is combined with a canterbury, or music rack; there seems to be no end to the variations of shape and size of this piece of furniture. It was every woman's delight and every housemaid's nightmare. Some were oblong in shape, serpentine or bow fronted, others triangular with twisted stems and daintily carved knobs, others again heart or kidney shaped. They were generally made of walnut, rosewood or fruitwoods. Their main feature is a series of graduated shelves supported by slim, turned pillars. The shelves themselves are sometimes inlaid with lighter woods, mother-of-pearl, ebony or ivory.

Beside a small sofa is a sofa table, a variation of a Pembroke table which can be brought out and placed in position when tea is served. Other items include a work table, with an inlaid top and underneath a fluted silk bag. There is also an embroidery frame on its carved stand and a small painting easel where the young ladies dabble in water-colours, and hidden away in a corner is a combined painting, writing and work desk, the daughter's little bit of privacy in a world where all women's lives had to be an open conspiracy. This desk has locked drawers and cupboards and in these she secretes innocent notes she has surreptitiously received from young men and the equally innocent valentines that arrive amidst a bustle of giggles and excitement each year on February 14th.

At a later period, desks have more elaborate cupboards and drawers and become heavily inlaid with ivory, ebony or mother-of-pearl. This type of desk would be painted black and highly polished, and often chairs and tables would be made to match this far too fussy piece of nonsense. I say nonsense because many of them were purely show pieces, too frail in construction to be of much practical use.

On one of the occasional tables lie copies of *The Gentlewoman's Magazine* and one of Mrs Gaugin's famous knitting books. These were specifically addressed to the ladies of the upper classes, though later Mrs Gaugin found that her works were not sufficiently appreciated by the gentlefolk and directed her later work to 'those women of humble origin who may take a delight in this simple craft'.

Later on Mrs Weldon's magazine might be found and even one or two of the heartwarming novels of Mrs Gaskell, Mrs Henry Wood or Mrs Molesworth.

The sitting room might well be said to symbolise the outward calm of the middle years of the era. Beyond its walls, in the fields and slums, down the mines and on factory floors could be heard murmurs of discontent. Engels had published *The Condition of the Working Class in England* in 1845, Karl Marx was working night and day at the British Museum on his revolutionary book, *Das Kapital* (1867), and a parson's wife was rebelling against the lot of women. Later she travelled the country extolling the virtues of atheism and scorning the claims of the religion in which she was born and nurtured. She was to lead the matchgirls of Bryant and May's into the first women's strike. Her name was Annie Besant and she was to be a pioneer of women's rights, birth control, free speech and Victorian Socialism. This dominant little woman thought and read herself into her iconoclastic position in the gentle and quiet seclusion of her Victorian sitting room.

85

85. Six-stemmed centrepiece, c. 1895. Pale yellow glass shading to blue with an opalescent effect. (Victoria and Albert Museum, London)

86. Writing, painting and work desk. Numerous drawers, cupboards and pigeon holes make this a useful if not a particularly elegant piece. A typical example of how the Victorian dream could easily turn into a nightmare. (Author's collection)

87. Papier-mâché tray and boxes. Papier mâché was developed in the 18th century as a cheap imitation of Oriental lacquer. The Birmingham firm of Jennens and Bettridge developed the technique of mother-of-pearl inlay in the 19th century and set the standard for decoration of the highest quality.
(Private collection)

88. French marble mantel clock. Black marble clocks adorned innumerable middle-class mantel-shelves from the mid century onwards. This example has the escapement on the face. (Private collection)

89. *The Lady Godiva Procession.* Thomas Stevens, a Coventry weaver, used the Jacquard loom to make multi-coloured woven silk pictures and ribbons. There has recently been a revival of interest in 'Stevengraphs'. (Private collection)

90. Samplers date back to the 17th century and died out in the late 19th century. Early Victorian examples usually have a little scene, the alphabet, a religious text, uplifting motto or verse, the child's name and the date, all embroidered on rough linen in a variety of stitches. In good condition the colours should not be faded, the stitches broken or the linen brittle, holed or discoloured. (Private collection)

88

The Lady Godiva Procession.

89

Preserve me Lord amidst the crowd
From every thought that's vain and proud
And raise my wand'ring eyes to see
How good it is to trust in thee

From all the enemies of truth
Do thou O God preserve my youth
And free my mind from worldly cares
From youthful sins and youthful snares

Lord in my heart though hard as stone
Let seeds of early grace be sown
Still water'd withthy heavenly love
Till they shall spring to joys above

Sarah Thomas workd This Sampler In the year of our Lord
1842 In the Eleventh year of her age

91. This pair of exquisite and unusual vases is characteristic of some of the best work by the New England Glass Company of about 1840. A pair of so-called 'witch balls' serve as covers, and the red, white and blue stripes, applied in the Venetian manner, add an air of festivity.
(The Metropolitan Museum of Art, New York, Edgar J. Kaufmann Charitable Foundation Fund)

92. Victorian silver-mounted bottles and boxes come in all shapes and sizes.
(Private collection)

93. Bone-china tea service by Spode, *c.* 1850. Bone china, made from china stone, china clay and calcine bone, was pioneered by the Spode company. Its combination of toughness and delicacy still ensures its popularity.
(Private collection)

94. Girandole candle-lustres in ruby and clear glass.
(Private collection)

91

92

93

94

95. Decorative panel worked in macramé.
(Victoria and Albert Museum, London)

96. Generally known as the 'conversational', the 'tête-à-tête'
or 'love seat', this example in laminated rosewood shows
the Victorians' ingenuity for inventiveness. It was made in
New York in the 1850s, possibly in the Belter factory. The
wood was curved with the help of steam and the decoration
is of finely carved flowers, leaves, vines, acorns and grapes.
(The Metropolitan Museum of Art, New York,
Gift of Mrs Charles Reginald Leonard, in memory of
Edgar Welch Leonard, Robert Jarvis Leonard,
and Charles Reginald Leonard)

95

96

97. Mid Victorian walnut tea table with turned legs and two drop leaves. The table would normally stand against the wall with its leaves down and be wheeled out on its castors when needed. The pleasant, unpretentious design shows that when the Victorians wished to do so they could produce good, honest work.
(Private collection)

98. Every detail of Victorian life was recorded in the furnishings of the dolls' house.
(Bethnal Green Museum, London)

97

98

THE LIBRARY

ET us now move along the hall, past the staircase to the room that is both a sanctum and a punishment cell, a place of study and a place of rest. This is the library, the master's domain. It has the kind of forbidding atmosphere which by its very nature demands that womenfolk shall keep out. Here the daily paper is kept and read, the weekly journals and monthly magazines are stored, and even those meant for the use of women must first pass male censorship. Here the sons and daughters are reprimanded if they have broken any of the 'thou shalt nots' laid down by the father. It is the temple dedicated to the Victorian narrow mindedness that was misnamed morality. It is the room where facile homage is paid to the world of literature. It is the office within the home where all personal business is transacted. If the need arose for a new hat or a new carpet the request would be met by, 'Come into the library, my dear, and talk it over'.

The first object that catches the eye as one enters the room is the massive desk with its chair in place behind it. The desk and chair are solidly made of stout oak with no concessions to either taste or aesthetic sensibility. The desk is purely a working surface with cupboards and drawers, and the chair an uncomfortable resting place giving neither ease nor comfort to its user. Library desks were usually of oak or mahogany, rarely in the finer timbers such as satinwood and walnut. On the desk is a large inkstand, made from a block of onyx with glass and Sheffield-plate containers for the ink and one or two quills.

In the centre of the longest wall is a bureau bookcase, a simple and direct statement of utility, lacking the panelling and inlay that gave such a perfect touch to its Georgian predecessor. Bookshelves line the rest of the walls, filled with leather-bound volumes all carefully selected for either their moral, edifying or cultural significance. There are volumes of sermons by 17th-

and 18th-century divines, books of poems by Wordsworth, Browning and by that dear man, so loved by the poor widowed Queen, Lord Tennyson. We might find the works of Thackeray and Trollope, books of devotion like Sir Thomas Browne's *Religio Medici*, or semi-fictitious historical horrifics like Foxe's *Book of Martyrs*. A few novels by the Brontë sisters and the works of Jane Austen have their place, but the novels of Mrs Gaskell, apart from *Cranford*, are absent, for she is a dangerous woman who is liable to spread the new ideas of social reform that are anathema to the average Victorian home of this class. As for that dreadful Mr Dickens who is writing those terrible things about the private schools, orphanages, workhouses and prisons, well, the man himself was an outlandish cad and his books certainly had no place in any gentleman's library. He had the audacity to challenge the right of the employer's use of child labour. He had the effrontery to suggest we ought to reform the prison system. He had outraged all decency by commenting on the wickedness of poverty. Had he not learnt that the poor are always with us, and, as Mrs Alexander's hymn rightly says, 'The rich man in his castle, the poor man at his gate, the high man and the lowly, God ordered their estate'.

It is quite likely that these books are seldom read; they are for show, the outward and visible sign of an inward and spiritual culture that the owner wishes to suggest to his visitors. Learning is dangerous, too much schooling is bad for everyone, and a strong element of ignorance is essential to the well-being of the body politic. This is the unwritten creed of most of the un-eminent Victorians.

The library chairs are plain and wholesome and the library steps, which, when folded, form a stool,

99. After the Great Exhibition of 1851, skeleton clocks became very popular. The intricate workings of this cathedral-type skeleton clock are framed by ornate metal scaffolding which is meant to resemble a Gothic cathedral. The whole should be encased in a glass dome which rests on the white marble base. (Private collection)

follow the same simple lines. The fact is that at this stage the laws of supply and demand control the designs and it is quicker and easier to turn out these plainer objects on a large scale than it is to produce more elaborate pieces of furniture. A folding-top card table is also to be found, and a games box which contains chessmen, draughts, counters, backgammon pieces, dice and several simple card games, together with the appropriate boards for playing these games on. A whisky decanter and matching Waterford cut-crystal glasses are hidden away in the corner cupboard, for it is in this room that intimate male friends of the family are talked to, reprimanded or entertained as the occasion demands. Suitors plead their cause and disclose their incomes or expectations, debtors appeal for grace and agree to a higher rate of interest, and servants are interviewed. Although the running of the house is primarily the wife's domain, the husband sees servants and approves their credentials, for an attractive maid is preferable in every way to a plain one.

In the library a large iron or steel cash box is carefully locked away and, towards the end of the century, one of the new household safes might be installed in this room. The walls are panelled to match the dining room, and the door is always kept locked except when in use and the key kept on the master's key ring.

A touch of luxury is added by a reading desk. This is tall and slim and has a sloping top with a ledge to rest the book upon. One always reads at it standing up, and this suggests that reading was not often indulged in, at least not here.

A swivelling oil lamp that can be either raised or lowered on its centre brass rod or turned in a circular movement until it gives the maximum light, stands on the library desk. Wall lights on wooden brackets and a large brass oil lamp on a small table complete the lighting in this room. Long windows with heavy velvet curtains look out on to the garden at the back of the house, but the curtains are often kept drawn in case the daylight should penetrate the musty atmosphere.

Stimulated by the wonders of the Great Exhibition and the dictates of fashion, the room undergoes several transformations during the sixty-odd years of Victoria's reign, scenes worthy of one of the popular Christmas pantomimes. The heavy, sombre panelling gets painted cream, the solid oak desk is replaced by a Chippendale reproduction with low-relief Chinese carving, and the chair by one with an upholstered leather seat to match the oblong of tooled leather that forms the top of the desk. Even the quills give way to penholders in bone, ivory or wood to hold the newly invented nibs. These had to be used with great care or blots of ink were spilt on the paper. Change and invention were the keynotes of the Victorian age and the furniture and fittings in a well-established Victorian home were never sacred.

We must also remember that the first public libraries were opened in 1850; Mudies had their subscription system for borrowing books, and those two authors whom grandfather would not have on his shelves, Mrs Gaskell and Charles Dickens, were now being avidly read by the new generation, and would lead many from the sentimental outlook of liberal Nonconformity to the more revolutionary thought of Christian Socialism. Father might lock his library door and forbid his family to read any books or magazines that had not passed his censorship, but he could not prevent the windows being slowly opened to let in first a gentle breeze then a tempestuous gale through the rooms and corridors of his crumbling castle. The fictitious Forsytes failed because, like Lot's wife, they could only look back. Likewise the Victorians wrecked their ship because they refused to trim its sails to the changing winds ushering in another age.

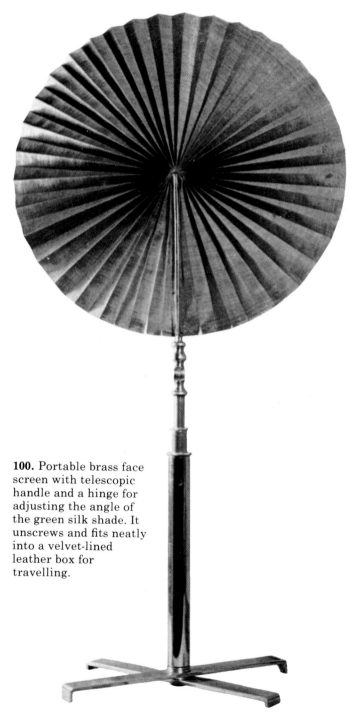

100. Portable brass face screen with telescopic handle and a hinge for adjusting the angle of the green silk shade. It unscrews and fits neatly into a velvet-lined leather box for travelling.

101. Glass paperweights. The two lower examples are the millefiori type. Above are two inexpensive scenic paperweights showing Yarmouth and Stonehenge; the third has a Christmas greeting.
(Private collection)

102. Mahogany pedestal desk made by Wright and Mansfield of Bond Street, London. The firm of Wright and Mansfield specialised in high-quality copies of 18th-century designs; Chippendale's pattern books were the source for this splendid desk.
(Private collection)

103. Strictly for the Victorian avant garde. A glass claret jug with silver mounts by Christopher Dresser, 1879–1880. (Victoria and Albert Museum, London)

104. Mahogany adjustable reading- cum candle-stand. (Private collection)

105. On the left: cut- and engraved-glass claret jug with ornate silver handle and pourer, 1855. On the right: green-glass American brandy decanter encased in silver. (Private collection)

106. American Gothic revival desk and bookcase made by J. and J. W. Meeks of New York. A superb piece in rosewood lined in satinwood and fitted with drawers, pigeonholes and a slanted writing surface. Note the elegant pointed arches and restrained decoration on the door panels. Few pieces of Victorian furniture achieved such a happy combination of design and craftsmanship. (The Metropolitan Museum of Art, New York, Rogers Fund)

104

105

88

106

THE CONSERVATORY & GARDEN

HE conservatory of our typical Victorian house is a jungle of potted plants. Heavily scented gardenias, camellias, calceolarias, geraniums, ferns and exotic palms stand on shelves from floor to ceiling each one in an elaborate plant holder called a jardinière. The jardinières are made in all shapes and sizes and from all kinds of materials: wrought iron, copper, bamboo, wood and Staffordshire pottery. The grandest have their own magnificent stands encrusted with ribbons, swags and other historical revival motifs, all of which vie with the plants for our attention. The tropical atmosphere is further evoked by a vine which trails across the domed glass roof. Everything flourishes under the careful surveillance of the gardeners. Heat is supplied from a solid fuel boiler and thick iron pipes running round the base of the conservatory. This was to give rise to the first form of central heating in the home. Japanese lanterns with candles or cleverly constructed oil lamps light the conservatory in the evenings. There are wrought-iron
109 tables and chairs, for on summer days tea might be served here. Here the croquet set and later the tennis nets and equipment might be stored. The noonday glory of an age of prosperity has arrived, and all who are able to indulge in it enjoy its luxury to the full.

As the century progresses gardens become increasingly popular. In well-to-do homes they are looked after by the gardeners, but towards the end of the century with the publication of various gardening books gardening is looked upon more as a hobby. Victorian gardens were less formal than in the 18th century; they were well tended with winding paths and flower beds and an abundance of evergreen shrubs, especially privet and laurel. There are shady nooks for picnics and chosen spots for statues, fountains and garden urns. Window boxes and hanging baskets prevail everywhere.

The 1860s might be looked upon as the high summer of an age. Let us then imagine a cloudless July afternoon in mid Victorian England in the quiet loveliness of the Victorian garden, the Marvel moment, 'annihilating all that's made, to a green thought in a green shade', has arrived. A fashionable private garden party is about to take place. Tables have been placed at the end of the lawn and on the terrace and are covered with spotless white, lace-trimmed cloths. Silver trays, 60 covered with doilies, are piled high with sandwiches, cakes, trifles in small glass dishes and other goodies to tempt the appetites of the guests. The mistress and her daughters walk idly about the garden waiting for their guests to arrive. Their dresses are of fine silks and velvets, high bodiced and flowing to trailing skirts at the rear, and they wear gloves of white kid or lace. Their parasols are of every hue: brown, green and blue silks, with matching or contrasting fringes, and handles of lacquered cane in colours to match the covers. Mother has her favourite parasol for the occasion. It is made of black silk with a lace border and is lined with maroon silk. Thrown over the top is a lovely canopy of Honiton lace. The handle is of carved ivory with silver mounts to suggest just that touch of opulence to her guests.

The servants bring out the china tea-cups and 93 matching plates of Worcester, Coalport and Copeland. On the tables are five- and six-stemmed vases in milk 85 glass or crystal carrying a wonderful array of exotic blooms from the hothouse, orchids perhaps, which, with the growing popularity of greenhouses, were being cultivated again as status symbols.

But death was soon to darken the halcyon days and drown an era in gloom. The Queen was to lose her beloved Albert and her odd way of life as the widow of Windsor was to set a new pattern over the land.

107. Flower vase in gilded apricot porcelain. Brown-Westhead, Moore and Company, 1870. The design of a white putto nonchalantly poised between two beribboned sheaths is in the Renaissance revival style.

91

108. Jardinière and stand. Brownfield, *c.* 1860. What could be more appropriate decoration for the bowl of a plant holder than the Death of a Roman Soldier and Gaius Mucius Scaevola burning off his left hand before Lars Porsena?

109

110

109. The fact that these cold, cast-iron branches could hardly have been comfortable to sit on, did not disturb the most discerning Victorian customer, whose love of rusticity conquered all. This example of a rustic chair is characteristically mid 19th-century in its naturalism—the branches and leaves are unmistakably those of an oak. (The Metropolitan Museum of Art, New York, Rogers Fund)

110. American imitation bamboo table and chair of the 1880s. In America imitation bamboo pieces were made almost entirely of maple but in Europe similar furniture was normally made of fruit woods. In a book of designs of 1876 a chair, not unlike the one seen here, was featured at $8·67. (The Metropolitan Museum of Art, New York, Anonymous Gift Fund)

111. Thonet's experimental bentwood furniture at London's International Exhibition of 1862.

112. Rosewood centre table, in the Rococo revival style, made by John Henry Belter between 1856 and 1861.

Belter had learned his trade in Württemberg, Germany, and came to New York in 1844. (Museum of the City of New York, Gift of Mr and Mrs Ernest Gunther Vietor)

111

112

The Bedroom

HE main bedroom, the one that belongs to the parents, has as its main item a large and ornate mahogany four-poster bed. This was the unspoken of, unwritten of, centre of marital life. Here take place the lying in when children are born and the laying out when the finality of death has taken place. On top of the bed is a
116 wonderful patchwork quilt, a wedding gift from the bride's mother and looked upon in many homes as a family heirloom. Victorian patchwork designs, made from odd scraps of materials from the ragbag, are fascinating. All are very colourful and some of the patternings are as elaborate as those on an Oriental carpet. The bed is hung with brocade and velvet hangings; later as beds become lighter and simpler in design the hangings are of muslin edged with lace or with folds of wide lace curtaining made at Nottingham.

At each side of the bed stand matching cabinets, with a small top drawer to hold oddments, and a cupboard beneath in which to keep the chamber pot, an essential part of every Victorian bedroom. The matching jug and basin, toothbrush holder, soap dish and slop
44 pail stand on a marble-topped washstand, made in mahogany to match the bed. These toilet sets were made by the finest makers of pottery in the country; Coalport, Minton, Wedgwood, Masons, and Doulton, all competed for the trade in these most useful household necessities.

The dressing table is my lady's domain and spells the word 'feminine' in its silver, crystal and porcelain fitments. On top is a long runner of Brussels lace. The patterns of Honiton, Buckingham and Brussels lace were later copied on lace-making machines but most homes were proud of their hand-made lace mats and runners. Standing in the centre of the dressing table is an oval tray, flanked by a pair of candlesticks. Pin
120 boxes, hair-tidies, ring-holders and pill boxes of silver,
81 crystal and porcelain stand alongside scent bottles in

cut crystal or coloured glass with silver covers to the stoppers. A small table with a wooden gallery, pierced to recapture the Chinese spirit of early Chippendale, serves masculine toiletry needs. On it stand his brushes **118** and combs, clothes brush and button-hooks, glass or Battersea pots for the various pomades that a gentle- **133** man uses for his hair.

On one of the bedside cabinets stands a repeater alarm, probably French, for Continental carriage clocks were very popular. On the other cabinet stands a night light, consisting of a pierced bronze or iron case with a removable lid and an engraved-glass front panel. Sometimes the other sides would have plain-glass panels and these would send a gentle and diffused light into the room. Fires were a hazard in the home and there were various forms of safety candlestick. For instance, the candle holder would be placed in a deep dish which was filled with water so that should the candle topple it would be immediately extinguished. There were some lovely designs in these candlesticks: delicate landscapes or sprays of flowers were used as decorations. not only were they useful and functional but showed in their shape a real feeling for simplicity.

Over a small and neat iron fireplace is a mantelshelf. On it stands a pair of nodding mandarins, an ornament that had become very popular in the middle sixties, and as a centrepiece is a splendid clock by the Sèvres or Dresden factories. On the walls are prints by Baxter, a sampler and silhouettes. The windows are **122,9** heavily draped with curtains to match those on the bed, and in addition are fitted with a coloured blind.

The next bedroom along the landing is used by the daughter. It is lighter and more frivolous than that of her parents. The bedroom suite is of painted wood, and instead of a patchwork quilt there is a frilled and flounced silk coverlet. Dainty chairs in painted woods inlaid with mother-of-pearl stand at each side of a

113. Wardrobe of Hungarian ash inlaid with purple wood. The piece was made by Holland and Sons in the late 1860s and cost £68 10s. (Private collection)

smaller dressing table, and the wardrobe is lighter than the heavy mahogany cupboard that stands in the parents' room, and has a large mirror fitted in the door. The bedside cabinets are of pine, painted and decorated, with basketwork sides, and on them are Botticelli-like angels by Copeland for candlesticks. The fittings on the dressing table are made of tortoiseshell, ivory, and papier mâché. Mother may be prudish but her daughters must be ultra feminine and have around and about them the essential fascination that makes them worthy 123 entries for the matrimonial stakes. Heart-shaped pincushions, crochetted hair-tidies, loop-knitted bedroom slippers, lavender-filled handkerchief sachets, all spell one word, 'charm'.

The son's bedroom tells quite another story. Here we find a brass bedstead with a heavy rug on it, a tallboy and wardrobe for his clothes, and a small table for shaving mirror and brushes. Sporting prints hang on the walls together with one or two of the naughtier 122 Baxter prints. This room is merely a place of sojourn, not of permanent habitation, for it was every young man's duty to find a wife, one whose dowry would assist him on his way to fortune even if fame were destined to elude him. On the mantel-shelf are Continental beermugs bought on a trip to Germany or Switzerland, and a piperack, filled with ornamental pipes that are never used. On the bedside table is a brass candlestick and a heavy alarm clock whose loud tick resounds all over the room.

The bedroom used by the governess is largely furnished with cast-offs from other rooms. A simple wooden or iron bedstead, a chest of drawers and a table with toilet mirror, a bedside cabinet and two ordinary chairs are all the furniture in the room. Clothes are kept in a built-in cupboard at the far side of the room. A servant, even one of their elevated rank, had no privacy. The duties of a governess kept her busy

for thirteen to fifteen hours a day. Her charges were her responsibility night and day and all she wanted to do when she reached her bedroom was to fall asleep.

Just as the other rooms undergo constant transformations and changes over the sixty-odd years of the Victorian age, so the bedrooms would be carried along in what was seen as a constant and endless stream of progress. The painted or heavily embossed French beds or their English copies would come and go, the bamboo moments would arrive and vanish, lacquer would have 110 its day and then go the same way as all its predecessors.

114. The prie dieu or kneeling chair, typical of High Church influence, was popular during the early and mid Victorian periods. This example has cross-stitch panels. (Private collection)

115. Honiton-lace fan with gilded mother-of-pearl ribs. Lace fans were a Victorian innovation; these delicate creations later gave way to the vulgar feather. (Private collection)

116. French workbox, c. 1860, which belonged to Mrs Benjamin H. Peabody of Pittsburgh, Pennsylvania, who made the patchwork quilt when in her eighties. (Private collection)

115

116

117. Crocodile dressing bag fitted with silver-gilt and chased toilet requisites, brushes and a clock. Advertisement in the *Illustrated London News*, 1898.

118. Gentleman's toilet mirror on a marble base. Compare its honest simplicity with the monstrosity on page 120. (Private collection)

119. The Xylonite Company pioneered the manufacture and use of plastics in consumer goods. Advertisement, 1893.

120. A delightful collection of small boxes for pills and keepsakes in an imaginative assortment of materials and designs. British and American. (Private collection)

121. German ticket clock. The Victorians thought of everything, even the digital clock. (Private collection)

122. Baxter print of the sculpture court at the Great Exhibition. In the 1830s George Baxter developed a process of cheap colour printing. His town and country scenes and views of the Great Exhibition which were bought by the masses are now much sought after by collectors. (Private collection)

123. A proposal card to soften the hardest heart. (Private collection)
Inside is a verse in the proposer's own hand:

Timorous when near, tho' bold when far away
I fain before you – my petition lay
Doubt not, I love you more at every meeting
I ask you to be mine, as time is fleeting
Oh 'say those words, all other words above
'I will be yours' then you the best I love.

121

122

123

THE NURSERY

ONE of the strangest aspects of the Victorian scene was the life led by middle-class children. They were brought up in complete ignorance of anything relating to sex. Most of the boys were looked upon and treated as eunuchs, and the girls were as jealously shielded from the world and guarded as were the Vestal virgins of earlier times. If Victorian morality was based on hypocrisy it was a very polite form that went under the pseudonym of 'good taste'. It might now be looked upon as humbug, but its purpose was to preserve that way of life to which it had pleased their idea of the Almighty to call them. Ignorance was more than bliss where the womenfolk were concerned: it was an essential part of good behaviour. Most Victorian girls had only two things to offer their husbands, their dowries and their virginity, and their husbands made the most of both.

Children were brought down to be inspected by mama each morning, they then spent the rest of the morning in the schoolroom with the governess. Lunch would be with the family if there were no guests, but if the parents were entertaining it would be served in the nursery where the nurse and governess would supervise their behaviour. The afternoon would again be passed doing lessons with an occasional period of play, but even play, if we are to judge by many children's games of the period had its educative and moral values.

Let us take a closer look at the cloistered world of the Victorian nursery. Since the nursery is also the
129,130 schoolroom, there are two or three davenports serving as desks. Slates, toys and games are stored in a large deal cupboard. The nursery also contains a bassinet for the youngest child and one or two beds for the younger members of the family. There is a chest of drawers for their clothes and perhaps a small wardrobe. The cots, for this is all the beds really were, are of painted pine with high sides to prevent the children falling out at

night. A small tin bath for the baby is kept here, while the older children would be taken to the bathroom to be washed. A few chairs and a table complete the furnishings. The walls are painted a dull green or an even duller blue, and on them are uplifting texts and framed samplers made by the older children. As the nurse **90** would spend quite a lot of her time here there is an easy chair for her and a high chair for the baby. On the **136** mantel-shelf are a few of her personal possessions, a cheap vase she had bought one day at the local fair, a **23,24** pair of small Staffordshire dogs that had come from her own home and which travelled with her from place to place. In one of the drawers are odd pieces of ribbon and scraps of lace she had been given by her mistresses all of which might come in handy one day if she were lucky enough to escape from domestic bondage and have a home of her own.

Standing in one corner, imposing itself over everything, is the dolls' house, the pride of every Vic- **57,98** torian nursery. This was not just a toy but a serious object to instil in the children the rudimentary elements of domesticity. Miniature furniture (not to be confused with travellers' samples that were also found **10,11** at this time), minute pots and tiny pans, stoves and kettles, fireplaces and cutlery, breakfast, dinner and tea services, all had their place in this home in miniature. Many of these were much more attractive than their full-sized counterparts, and were made by the best-known factories and potteries.

On the table is a popular game called floral lotto **127** which is really a form of what we know today as bingo. Cards were handed out that were divided into sections, each containing a picture of a flower; oval counters were then drawn, on which were printed the Latin, English and common names of flowers. The idea was to cover the card with the corresponding counters. There are also jigsaw puzzles and elementary wooden blocks that can be made into pictures. These are of various topics like the Kings and Queens of England, in chronological order and with added historical references.

124. Children's toys. Butcher's shop, *c.* 1850.
(Bethnal Green Museum, London).
English wax doll in fashionable walking costume
of *c.* 1880. (The London Museum).
Tammany bank, an American mechanical cast-iron
money bank. (Pollock's Toy Museum, London)

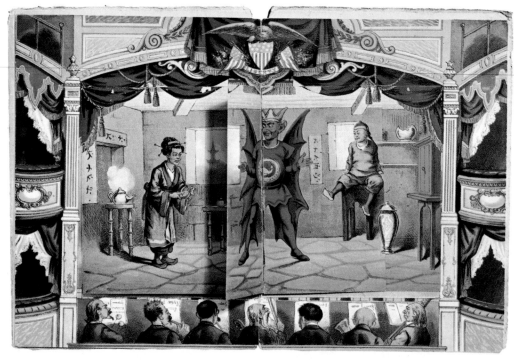

125. Colourful American
picture book of *Aladdin*.
The plot unfolds as you
turn the pages.
(Private collection)

126. China doll. Much care was lavished on the production of Victorian dolls. This elegant young lady in taffeta and lace rides in an equally elegant pram. (Private collection)

127. Table of children's games: a doll in a cot, Grandall's District School, books, penny toys, floral lotto and an elementary jigsaw of the Kings and Queens of England. (Private collection)

127

128. German straw-work ark and its patient painted-wood occupants. The flat-hatted human figures are traditional in design. (Private collection)

129,130. Davenport in walnut shown both closed and open. These small writing desks originating from the 18th century remained popular throughout the Victorian period. They are relatively expensive today and made-up versions abound. (Collection S. A. Pollitt Esq.)

128

129

130

On the wall is a wonderful device from America to illustrate the story of mankind. The history is written in some detail then mounted on two rollers, one at each side of the frame. As the rollers are turned, the story of mankind is unfolded, from the beginning to the present. This amazing plaything was made by Jay Andrews, Decker and Company of Chicago. Also from America is Grandall's District School, patented in 1867, consist- **127** ing of wooden blocks to be made into pictures.

In the toy cupboard are more educational games such as Learning to Read the Hard Way, a cabinet containing drawers of cardboard letters and words. The child has to build up a page as in a book and so ease the way to reading. There are various aids to teaching including, for instance, A Compendium of Botany exhibited by the improved phantasmagoria lantern, book and hand-painted slides included.

In lighter vein is the popular card game Happy Families. Many and loud were the screams of delight over Mr Bun the Baker and his contemporaries. A variation of this is a box of wooden blocks with heads, arms and legs on separate blocks. These could be rearranged to create strange and bewildering creatures. There is a box of penny toys ranging from a horse on a **127** spring, which when depressed can be made to gallop, to a zoetrope, a circular series of pictures of the same figure but in slightly different positions; when the circle was whirled round the figure seemed to be walking, running, dancing or doing strange acrobatics. Here in a child's penny toy we have the beginnings of the fortunes of Metro-Goldwyn-Mayer. Another amusing game is Spooner's Changing Drolleries; these consisted of a picture with one or several holes. By rotating a disc behind it is possible to change the scene which appears in the hole, like putting different heads on the same body, some gay, some grave, some gruesome. A popular theme shows the animals entering Noah's Ark.

The pride of every nursery is the wax doll. This is **124** seldom if ever played with and was often kept in a glass case only to be brought out on very special occasions. The other dolls are made of wood or rags, while among the more expensive kinds are those with pottery heads, legs and arms; some of these are dressed in the same manner as mama. To go with the doll is a doll's pram, made of wood and leather with buttoned up- **126** holstery, a folding canopy, and a wicker-work cradle.

Among other toys is a much abused rocking horse, a Noah's Ark in straw work so fine that it looks **128** like a piece of Tunbridge ware, and a hansom cab. **151**

We even find the beginnings of what later was played by adults and called Shove Halfpenny. This is a game called Squails and is played with large and small bone counters with decorative centres. There is also cap and ball, Diabolo and tiddlywinks to while away the idle hours.

Finally there are the books. Victorian children's **125** books are either pedantically enlightening and edifying or charmingly written and illustrated fairy stories. In our nursery alphabet books, moral rhymes and cautionary tales are much in evidence.

131. Before the phonograph came the polyphon. Metal discs played the latest popular tunes, c. 1880. (Private collection)

132. The forerunner of the motion-picture. A red tin magic lantern with cellofilm strip pictures, 1890. (Percy Band Collection, Metropolitan Toronto and Region Conservation Authority)

ATTIC & BELOW STAIRS

S the archpriestess of middle-class morality and over-feeding Mrs Beeton has told us, servants were the status symbol of the typical Victorian family. In her famous *Book of Household Management* she has worked out for us the economics of this to perfection. Those with incomes of about £1,000 a year should employ a cook, upper housemaid, nursemaid, an under housemaid and a manservant; about £750 a year, a cook, housemaid, nursemaid and footboy; about £500 a year, a cook, housemaid and nursemaid. The same authority gives a detailed scale of wages paid round about 1861 for separate servants with board and lodging, and uniform, 'livery' as Mrs Beeton calls it with that innate touch of snobbery that runs throughout her book. 'A cook, £14 to £30 a year; a housekeeper, £20 to £45; upper housemaid, £12 to £20; under housemaid, £9 to £12; kitchenmaid £9 to £14; and nursemaid £8 to £12 a year.' If the household was fortunate enough to have a butler, he could earn £25 to £50 a year. We must remember that working hours were unlimited, time off as little as one night each week and then you had to be in before ten in the evening, and one day off a month if you were lucky.

The servants lived at the top of the house. Furnishings were scant: a painted deal chest of drawers and table, iron bedsteads with straw mattresses, an iron washstand in the corner with an enamel jug, bowl and soap dish. The housekeeper and cook might have a cast-off wardrobe or cupboard in their bedroom, but the other servants had to keep their clothes and personal belongings in a box which they pushed under the bed. Life below stairs was controlled by a table of precedence as dogmatic as that laid down by Debrett. The constant conflict between cook and housekeeper was a byword in every establishment and presented its own particular problems to the servants. If they supported the housekeeper the cook would see they got poorer meals, while if they upheld the cook's claims to superior status the housekeeper would give them extra work to do. If there was a butler then the cook and housekeeper vied for his favours, and heaven help anyone else who dared to flirt with him.

There were grates to be cleaned out and black **139** leaded, fires to be laid and ashes to be riddled so that the larger pieces of clinker could be used again on the kitchen fire. There was endless polishing of silver and brass, preparing and cooking food, washing up after meals, and the heating and carrying of water to the bedrooms of family and guests. Dusting, scrubbing, washing, polishing, these were the day-to-day tasks that kept the servants on the go from dawn to dusk.

Comfort was not the hallmark of their lives. They sat on plain deal chairs, later bentwood ones, that **111** were far from comfortable. They ate off bare boards on the daily scrubbed kitchen table, and the only lights they were allowed were tallow candles; the number of these would be rationed lest they were tempted to stay up late and thus also to rise late in the morning. All the laundry would be done at home. Sheets had to be washed, table linen to be kept spotless. In the laundry **134** would be two or three washtubs, an old fashioned coal fired boiler, scrubbing boards and brushes, clothes dollies, maidens and a wringer. Along one wall would **137** be the ironing table and on a shelf just above it the irons, flat irons for ironing, pleating, goffering and curling, all essential if the starched frills and furbelows were to be kept neat and tidy.

The nursemaid would be expected to keep both baby and its napkins and clothes clean, and the butler,

133. Decorative pot lids of the Prince Consort, Shrimping, the Great Exhibition, a Wayside Inn, Derby Day and the Queen at Wimbledon, July 2nd, 1860. Multi-coloured transfer-printed lids were made for vessels which originally contained pomades, fish pastes or potted shrimps. The collector should look out for the brilliant colours and fine crazing which characterise the genuine article. (Private collection)

a euphemism for a man of all work, was expected to press and clean his master's clothes as often as they needed attention. It is true that some of the work would be sent out to a washerwoman but the housekeeper was instructed to keep this down to a minimum and as much as possible was done at home.

141,144 The kitchen dresser is of pine. In it the kitchen cutlery and cooking utensils are kept while on the shelves are thick pottery cups, saucers and plates that are used for the servants' meals. The scullery walls
146 have lines of shelves with kettles, frying pans, fish kettles, heavy iron saucepans, gleaming copper pans and cooking pots of all sizes, and in the pantry marble shelves and open ventilators to keep the food cool. Here in the kitchen you might find one or two cheap ornaments. Goss cottages, pottery figures of the royal family, or garish groups of gypsies or one of the white
140 and gold splattered pieces of late Staffordshire, a favourite being *Darby and Joan*, or, in a more rakish mood, three tottering Scotsmen looking rather bewildered, the caption reading *Auld Lang Syne*. You
23,24 might find fairings, gifts from the milkman or grocer's boy, *The Last in Bed puts out the Light* or *Returning Home at Three in the Morning* or for the more timid *A Mouse, a Mouse*.

The servants were as fond of knick-nacks as their employers. Among their possessions were pottery pin boxes in the form of dressing tables, some complete with mirrors, or trinket boxes with dogs, cats or groups of children on the lids. Match strikers and spill holders, these covered an endless variety of domestic episodes from a girl minding the geese to a man about to embark on a journey. These things although trivia in themselves showed how the working classes had the same acquisitive instincts as their employers. The middle-class young woman looked for a husband who could offer her a home of her own equal, while the working girl hoped for the grocer, the milkman, the coalman or baker, to make her his wife and allow her to exchange one kind of drudgery for another.

134

134. Linen cupboard stacked with real linen sheets and tablecloths, starched and ironed to perfection. Every item was edged with lace, crotchet or drawn-thread work, all done by hand.

135. The brass bedstead was one more cleaning nightmare for the harassed chambermaid.

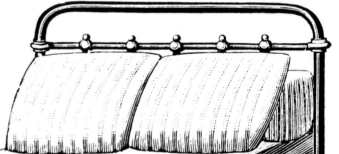

135

136. Adjustable baby chair. Illustrated in an 1892 edition of *Furniture and Decoration*. The Victorians loved ingenious multi-purpose objects. This chair can be used as a high chair, a rocking chair, and a mobile baby carriage.

137. Cast-iron wringer or mangle. It took a sturdy lass to wring dry the weekly wash.

138. Many of Singer's Victorian sewing machines are still giving good service.

139. Cast-iron fire grate.

140

140. Victorian named and unnamed Staffordshire figures. Early Victorian pieces followed the tradition of earlier potters like Walton and Wood. After about 1880, production generally became coarser. Type of clay, colours, texture and glaze are all pointers to age and value. (Author's collection)

141. Brown salt-glazed stoneware jugs decorated with raised hunting scenes, windmills and men smoking and drinking. Popular throughout the 19th century, these jugs were originally used for serving hot punch since they retain the heat so efficiently. (Private collection)

142. Wedgwood kitchenware in plain creamware, also known as Queen's ware. Wedgwood continued to produce 18th-century designs throughout the Victorian period. Victorian creamware is, however, darker and coarser than earlier pieces. The twin dishes in the foreground are sweetmeat baskets.

141

143

144

143. A splendid dish to whet the appetite.

144. Gadgets galore. A selection of Victorian kitchen utensils including jelly and aspic moulds, butter printers, a mould for making soft cheeses, a spice box complete with nutmeg grater, tea canisters, a steak bat and a food warmer. This type of food warmer contained a night light which kept warm a comforting spiced drink on a cold winter's night. (Private collection)

145

145. Railroad flask. American commemorative whisky flask of mould-blown glass showing a horse-drawn railroad car and with the inscription *Success to the Railroad*. These flasks–full or empty–are much sought after today. (Private collection)

146

146. And for thirsty stay-at-homes, a particularly elegant mid century copper kettle with a brass swinging handle. (Private collection)

Conclusion:
What is VICTORIANA?

Y the 1890s the Victorian age was drawing to a close. The Queen had another ten years on the throne. The Diamond Jubilee was to win her once more the acclaim of her loyal subjects as she rode in triumph through the London she disliked so intensely. As she sat in her carriage on that festal day she thought of dear Albert, of honest John Brown, of the quiet groves of Windsor Park and the peaceful solitude of Balmoral. 'How kind, how very kind', she murmured, but her heart was not here, not in these crowded streets, not with the tumultuously applauding multitudes who had gathered to give her a hail and, as many of them also knew, a farewell. Her thoughts were at Osborne. How Albert had loved it. For her it now became the one place where she felt nearest to his Shade.

The fact is that the people were getting a little tired of the moral restrictions of the age. They had become satirical about its platitudes. They were fighting to get out of its prison house and into the freedom they saw waiting for them in the Edwardian age. The scandalous life of the Prince of Wales, even now he had the lovely Alexandra by his side, was still the talking point of the clubroom and four ale bar alike. His mother had lived too long, and kept him in the background too much, so why blame him if he did try to kick over the traces now and then.

The operas being presented at the Savoy Theatre by Mr D'Oyly Carte, the works of those clever men Mr Gilbert and Mr Sullivan, were a subtle protest against an age that had dragged on too long, and the plays of Mr Wilde were all tilting at the moral strictures of a period that placed conformity before principle and manners before morality. The voices of dissent were being heard all over the country, and the newly emerging trade unions were beginning to make demands for the rights of the working man. A few women's voices were also heard in protest against their lack of rights, an indecency that trampled on their dignity and kept them as the mere chattels of men. Progress, a doubtful word to apply to any phase of human endeavour, had been the rallying cry of the Victorians. They saw the development of the postal services and transport, and the promise of the horseless carriage as milestones on the way, if not to heaven, to at least as near to it as men could go. Wages had risen a little and the working man was able to afford a few luxuries, cheap glass, tawdry ornaments, souvenir items from seaside resorts that made him feel that Jack was as good as his master. The rise of the Victorian era was marked by the steady increase in the ownership of goods and chattels, and the decline of the same age was marked by the increase of the nasty, the common, and the vulgar: it is of these things that most people think when we mention the word, Victoriana.

What then is Victoriana? The simple answer is that there is no such animal. It is an eclectic name for the good, bad and indifferent things that were produced during the sixty-odd years of the Queen's reign. The good were the few, the bad were the many, and the indifferent were the thousand and one things in between. The root of the trouble is that there was no Victorian age in the same sense that there had been an Elizabethan, Jacobean, Georgian or a Regency age. Each of these had an innate unity and this was reflected in the creative outlook of the architects, furniture-makers, potters, glassmakers and gardeners of the time. All worked to a common end, and that end was to say simply and quietly that this is the best as we see it and it is all part of a considered whole.

147. Commemorative goblet celebrating the British victory in the Transvaal War, 1899–1900. The goblet typifies British Imperial pride. Utterly convinced of their divine mission, the great British nation had once again crushed the foreign usurper. A decorative piece of nostalgia. (Private collection)

152

Let us now return to a typical Victorian room and see how this lack of an inner vision, giving an integrity to the whole, manifests itself. A large and **20** ornate sideboard is the first object that meets the eye. On it stands an alabaster clock with ornaments to match, looking like miniature tomb sculptures, and a silver tray and tea service, bought firstly for its weight **154** and secondly for its over-elaborate ornamentation. The chairs are lighter, and are obviously copied from Hepplewhite, but again have been given that strange bow-legged housemaid's knee look that we find on so much Victorian furniture. There is a fine satinwood table, at first sight very lovely, a golden honey colour inlaid with lighter and darker woods around its narrow border. On top of it, in a much heavier style, is an oval-fronted cabinet, a drawer beneath and glass-cased cupboards above. One wonders why it has been placed on the table, but it is part of it: a sliding flap turns out to form a writing desk. In an earlier age this idea would have been interpreted to incorporate a stationery cabinet as part of the table, and carefully designed and proportioned to fit into a scheme as a whole. This present table, writing desk, cabinet, only succeeds in making the worst of three worlds and adding a touch of moneyed vulgarity to a piece of furniture. There is another satinwood table, with a hexagonal top and inlays; the legs are well proportioned and stand like slender willows. Here is perfection, but we are not allowed to see the top or enjoy the shape for a heavy velvet cover lies over it, and standing on it is a jardinière in rather garish colours. The simple statement that the table makes has been lost in the vulgar guffaws of the offensive plantpot.

In the corner is a whatnot with five graduated shelves, at each of the corners of the shelves a pagoda-shaped wooden knob. Each shelf is covered with objets d'art, those useless but often expensive presents so loved by this money-satiated generation. A delicate papier-mâché box lies next to a shell-encrusted container with 'Mother' picked out in tiny shells along the front. Cheap copies of Meissen bandsmen stand side by side with an exquisite Dresden shepherdess. The whatnot is in burr walnut but hardly any of its surfaces can be seen for it is cluttered with a hundred and one pieces and looks like a stall at a village jumble sale.

The next item our eyes alight on is a tea table. It is rosewood and has curved legs which form a billowing front when the flap is closed and the table stands against the wall. On it is a lace cloth and set out is a tea **43** service from either the Derby or Worcester factories, but in spite of the fine quality of the china there is too much gold and too many colours in the patterning. Should this table be used for afternoon tea, the lace cloth and tea service will be removed and an embroidered cloth, 'My daughter's work, you know she is so clever with her needle', brought out, and even finer eggshell china laid for the tea to be served in. The teaspoons are a little on the large side, a heavier copy of a Georgian pattern, and you may, if the hostess has only recently acquired them, be asked to feel the weight.

There are several oil lamps in the room, one by Minton, another by Masons, and probably one with a coloured cut-glass bowl. These were mainly used as ornaments for the new gas light had been installed. Before the invention of the incandescent mantle, gas light had an open flame, shielded from draughts by glass bowls; these were sometimes in the form of water lilies, or tulips, or engraved with pastoral scenes. Nothing was complete in itself, and everything had to have something added to it to give it the right place in its period. There are beaded footstools, cross-stitch fire- **84** screens, wax flowers, miniatures, Tunbridge ware boxes and water-colours. Just as the wasp waist, the high bust and well proportioned bustle meant that you carried all before and behind you as you sauntered through the rooms, so those rooms themselves had everything on show. In spite of the stern words of Mr Ruskin and the quiet tones of William Morris the Victorians suspected beauty in any form except their own. There was something immodest in enjoyment, immoral in beauty, and intrinsically evil in good taste. The result was that with a few rare exceptions everything was a compromise.

In order to show how decadence overtook design I would like to consider the appearance of the toilet mirror, an essential item of bedroom furniture from the late 17th century to the present day. Sheraton visualised this as a light mirror, shaped as a shield, or oval or oblong, with a rounded top and made mainly in a lovely

148. Souvenir rose envelope showing scenes from Shakespeare's *Richard II* as performed at the Princess Theatre, Oxford Street, London, 1887. (Victoria and Albert Museum, London)

149. Irresistible play-bill of *c.* 1850 advertising a thrill-packed drama of piracy and romance. Will Captain Grunter force Julian to walk the plank? What respectable Victorian could resist such suspense. (Victoria and Albert Museum, London)

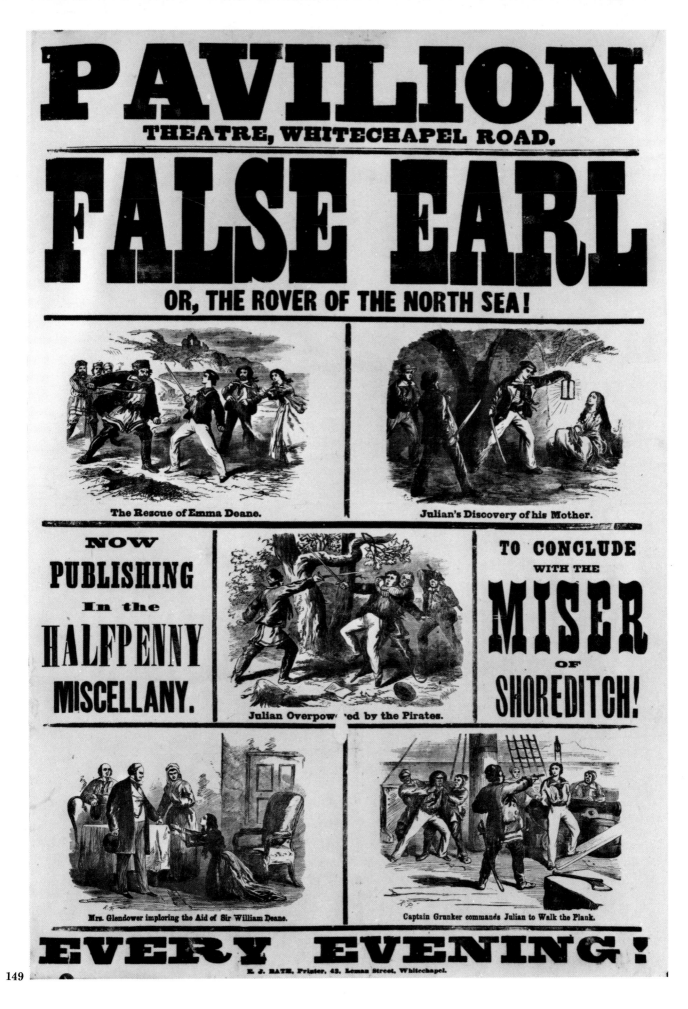

The Rescue of Emma Deane.

Julian's Discovery of his Mother.

Julian Overpowered by the Pirates.

Mrs. Glendower imploring the Aid of Sir William Deane.

Captain Grunker commands Julian to Walk the Plank.

PAVILION
THEATRE, WHITECHAPEL ROAD.
FALSE EARL
OR, THE ROVER OF THE NORTH SEA!

NOW PUBLISHING In the HALFPENNY MISCELLANY.

TO CONCLUDE WITH THE MISER OF SHOREDITCH!

EVERY EVENING!

E. J. BATE, Printer, 43, Lemas Street, Whitechapel.

149

150. Toilet glass from the Great Exhibition, 1851. The *Art Journal* described the piece as being 'of rare taste in conception, and of great merit in execution'.

151. Tunbridge-ware boxes, paper knife, compass and thermometer. Thousands of tiny pieces of different coloured woods make up the inlaid mosaic pictures on Tunbridge-ware articles. Originally a block of wood strips is produced – like Blackpool rock – from which thin slices of mosaic veneer are cut. The technique was perfected early in the century, and quantities of small objects were produced for an appreciative public for whom the intricate craftsmanship held a special appeal. (Private collection)

152. Sir W. S. Gilbert's drawing room. Gilbert and Sullivan's comic operas brazenly debunked the British Establishment, much to the delight of the middle classes. Few suspected that Gilbert's wit concealed a Dickensian social conscience. His drawing room, indeed, with its neo-Renaissance fireplace, ornaments and aspidistra, is a shrine to bourgeois opulence.

honey coloured mahogany. The frame would be delicate, serpentine fronted with one or two drawers keeping to the essential lightness of the general design. Chippendale might go in for a rather more ornate mounting, but again lightness was his objective. Small brass ornaments would decorate the two pillars, the swivel pins and tiny knobs to the drawers in matching mounts. Later the mirror grew larger but the frame

118 would be in perfect proportion giving the same light look to the finished product. More drawers were added, in the centre and at the side. They were never obtrusive or top heavy, but always had an innate elegance and refinement. Let us compare this with examples from

150 the mid 19th century. The frames have become heavy, the drawers are much larger with bulging fronts. The neat swivel pins have been replaced by large and clumsy wooden knobs. Some are so large that they completely overpower with their weight and garishness. Some have brass candle-holders fitted to the sides of the frame. The same decadence of design applied to the worst Victorian furniture. It was too heavy, too ornate, and over elaborate in decorations, be they in inlays or carvings.

140 Let us take another example, Staffordshire pottery figures. The earlier ones made by Wood and Walton, inspired to a certain extent by pieces of Chinese porcelain that had recently come into this country, were soft in colouring, delicate in design and a delight to gaze upon. Compare this with a figure of Shakespeare made about 1860, the stance is awkward, the modelling clumsy, the appearance heavy, and the colouring garish. What caused this decline? Simply the laws of supply and demand. The earlier figures were bought by the wealthier classes who wanted quality and not mere quantity from their craftsmen. Not so the moneyed classes of the Victorian period. When they wanted anything they wanted it yesterday and were not prepared to wait until tomorrow. The result was that inferior potters turned out thousands of poorly conceived pieces simply to enable Messrs Smith to keep up with Messrs Jones.

Throughout the period there were rebels, outsiders, from Morris to Beardsley. As a result of their influence there is a current of original, progressive design which runs through Victorian decorative arts. But, alas, it is the exception and not the rule. That is why when we see an ugly or a ridiculous piece of furniture or objet d'art our first reaction is that it is Victorian. Eventually the rebel theories of art and design turned the tables on the upholstered vulgarity of popular Victorian taste.

For today's collector, the mass of available Victoriana offers the lure of an unexplored treasure chest. Yet before succumbing to temptation it would be wise to remember the standards set by the great designers of the past: Chippendale, Adam, De Lamerie, Wedgwood. Theories of beauty and taste are never constant, but good design outlives them. Victoriana, is it a term of praise or abuse? Time alone will give us the true answer.

153. Regency tea caddy with Victorian decoration added. The Victorians, like nature, abhorred a vacuum. In this case, a plain tea caddy with lion's-head handles has been spoiled with crudely engraved floral swags. Incidentally, tea caddies were always locked, since tea was a very expensive luxury. (Private collection)

154. Fanciful silver teapot designed by J. H. Powell. Maker's mark, John Hardman and Company, Birmingham, 1861. Powell was a pupil of the Gothic-revivalist architect A. W. N. Pugin, who designed the decoration of the Houses of Parliament. (Victoria and Albert Museum, London)

155. Electroplated tea service by Christopher Dresser, 1880. While most designers were thinking of decoration, Dresser thought of function and of the significance of mass-production. It is scarcely credible that this innocuous tea service was once considered revolutionary. Dresser was a pioneer of modern design; as such his work has a special interest for the collector.
(Victoria and Albert Museum, London)

153

154

155

156.
Queen Victoria and her dog
by William Nicholson, 1897. Coloured wood engraving.
A stark, compassionate portrayal of the old Queen in the year
of the Diamond Jubilee. Nicholson, famous for his
woodcuts of Victorian characters, was also a pioneer of
British poster design.
(British Museum, London)

157.
Purple velvet encases Queen Victoria's funeral service book.
(Private collection)

'Dust to dust, and ashes to ashes,
Into the tomb the Great Queen dashes.'

Thus was Victoria, Queen and Empress, mourned by one of
her loyal subjects, an anonymous Indian village poet.
One can almost hear the ghostly reply,
'We are not amused'!

Index

ACKNOWLEDGEMENTS

The author would like to express his thanks to Messrs Sidgwick and Jackson for permission to quote from John Drinkwater's poem *Birthright*; to Mr Clive Wainwright of the Victoria and Albert Museum, London; to Mr A. Malcolm of the American Museum in Britain; to Kenneth and Kate Taylor of Curry Rivel; to Mr Purchase of Taunton; to Mr W. Mullen of Stogumber; to Mr and Mrs Cotton; and to Mr Don Ross, President of the British Musical Society.

He would also like to express his special thanks to Mr Anthony Pegrum without whose invaluable assistance this book would not have been possible.

SOURCES OF PHOTOGRAPHS

LAMPS.   LAMPS.   MAPL

Very Handsome and Massive Electro-Bronzed Lamp, with Loose Container, Duplex Burner, Extinguisher, Ornamental Globe and Chimney complete. **£1 12 6.**

Candle Shades in Paper, Linen, and Silk.

In an immense Variety of Styles and colours.

From 2½d. each.

Handsome Electro-Bronzed Duplex Lamp, fitted with Extinguisher, loose Container, moulded Opal Globe and Chimney complete. **18s. 6d.**

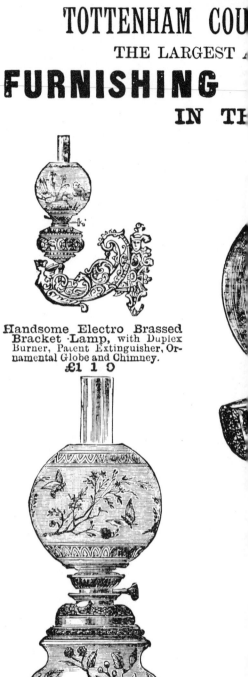

Handsome Electro Brassed Bracket Lamp, with Duplex Burner, Patent Extinguisher, Ornamental Globe and Chimney. **£1 1 0**

Squat Duplex Lamp, in Ivory China, with Blue Decoration, Loose Container, Lever-Action Burner and Extinguisher, Opaline Shade and Chimney complete. **14s. 6d.**

Handsome Decorated China Duplex Lamp, with Solid Brass Supports, Loose Container, best Lever-Action Burner, with Extinguisher, Ornamental Globe and Chimney complete. **£1 12 6.**

The Patent "Belge" Lamp, 42-candle power, in Handsomely Decorated China, with Bronzed Foot, Ornamental Globe and Chimney complete. **£1 17 6**

A great variety of different Patterns in Stock.

Hands
Corin
with
Duplex
guish
Chim